The Allure of the Archives

The Lewis Walpole Series in Eighteenth-Century Culture and History

The Lewis Walpole Series, published by Yale University Press with the aid of the Annie Burr Lewis Fund, is dedicated to the culture and history of the long eighteenth century (from the Glorious Revolution to the accession of Queen Victoria). It welcomes work in a variety of fields, including literature and history, the visual arts, political philosophy, music, legal history, and the history of science. In addition to original scholarly work, the series publishes new editions and translations of writing from the period, as well as reprints of major books that are currently unavailable. Though the majority of books in the series will probably concentrate on Great Britain and the Continent, the range of our geographical interests is as wide as Horace Walpole's.

Arlette Farge

The Allure of

the Archives

Translated by Thomas Scott-Railton

Foreword by Natalie Zemon Davis

Yale UNIVERSITY PRESS

New Haven & London

Published with assistance from the Annie Burr Lewis Fund, and from the foundation established in memory of Philip Hamilton McMillan of the Class of 1894, Yale College.

Yale University Press books may be purchased in quantity for educational, business, or promotional use. For information, please e-mail sales.press@yale.edu (U.S. office) or sales@yaleup.co.uk (U.K. office).

Designed by Lindsey Voskowsky.
Set in Adobe Caslon type by IDS Infotech, Ltd.
Printed in the United States of America.

The Library of Congress has cataloged the hardcover edition as follows:
Farge, Arlette.
    [Goût de l'archive. English]
The allure of the archives / Arlette Farge ; translated by Thomas Scott-Railton ; foreword by Natalie Zemon Davis.
        pages   cm. — (Lewis Walpole series in eighteenth-century culture and history)
    Originally published as Le Goût de l'archive. Editions du Seuil, 1989. Collection La Librairie du XXIe siècle sous la direction de Maurice Olender.
    Includes bibliographical references.
    ISBN 978-0-300-17673-5 (alk. paper)
    1. Archives. I. Scott-Railton, Thomas. II. Davis, Natalie Zemon, 1928– III. Title.
CD953.F3713 2013
944.04—dc23   2012048869

    ISBN 978-0-300-19893-5 (pbk.)

A catalogue record for this book is available from the British Library.

10 9 8 7 6 5 4 3 2 1

Contents

Foreword

Readers of Arlette Farge's writings have marveled at the world of eighteenth-century France that she has opened before our eyes. Whether in her stylish and lyrical French or in excellent English translation, her books have brought to life women and men of Paris in their workshops, bedrooms, and kitchens; on their doorsteps and in their streets and taverns; making appeals to their parish church and summoned before the commissariat of police. She has retrieved stories of love and abandonment among young working people and servants; of quarrels between apprentices and masters, with the master's wife standing in the middle; of street crowds gawking at neighbors, or watching executions or fireworks, or marching in vigorous protest. She has helped us hear the sounds of popular Paris life: the timbre of songs sung mockingly in front of an employer's door or chanted sorrowfully at a funeral procession; the slogans of protest and the groans of suffering. She has caught the rumors afloat among the people, the news accounts printed and spread about anything from royal doings to the cost of bread, and showed how these coalesced into a form of "public opinion."

Whether portraying an out-of-work baker so poor he was reduced to stealing bread to eat (as in her earliest publication) or quoting a jealous suitor insulting his would-be bride at a local fair (as in a recent work), Arlette Farge writes with respect for the human qualities of her subjects and a wise appreciation for the range in their feelings, from rage, cruelty, and sorrow to audacity, solidarity, and love. Eighteenth-century life in France is "fragile," as she says in the title of one of her most celebrated books, but it is also full of possibility. I had the delight of seeing this generous vision in play when we served as co-editors of the early modern volume of *A History of Women in the West*.

The remarkable achievement of Arlette Farge has been especially drawn from a vast judicial archive, the criminal records of the Préfecture of Paris, a court of first instance, and of the police of Paris. The outreach of the lieutenant general and the commissioners of the police was a crowning achievement of the Ancien Régime structures of authority: complaints, arrests, trials for petty offenses, prisons, networks of spies eavesdropping on the inhabitants of Paris, and much more. Farge's first book using such sources, *Délinquance et criminalité: Le Vol d'aliments à Paris au XVIIIe siècle*, became an instant classic in the social history of crime, its detection, and prosecution: who stole food? where? what? why? and what happened to them?

But already here Arlette Farge saw that though these documents were framed around legal prosecution and defense, much else could be gleaned from them about the life, feeling, and language of the poor and vulnerable. So over the years, as she made her trips to the Archives Nationales and the Archives de la Bastille at the Arsenal Library and other collections, Farge read these police records with and against the grain: for the legal narrative of accuser and accused, but also for what was revealed beyond that narrative. An example of her keen eye is her 2003 book, *Le Bracelet de parchemin*, where she explores the bits of paper sometimes attached to the bodies of those found frozen or drowned or otherwise deceased in the waters and by-ways of Paris and its environs—their "parchment bracelets" and also other writings on them or collected in inquiries about them. She describes herself coming upon such a bracelet from 1761 and reading the police description of its contents: a cross, a heart, and letter/number E 184. On other bodies were shirts, handkerchiefs, and cravats with initials embroidered on them—"A.D.," "D.F.," "G.P."—as well as garments whose color spoke to the taste of the deceased. From these and other signs and papers, Farge gives us a new way to think of how eighteenth-century French people marked their identity.

In *The Allure of the Archives*, elegantly translated for us by Thomas Scott-Railton, Arlette Farge takes us into the archives and pulls us into the experience of research. Specifically, we're at Arsenal library, where the police archives are held and where the reading room can be glacially cold on winter days. Farge takes us through the confusion of getting a reader's card, having the required identification, finding the right office, knowing where to line up for a seat in the reading room, discovering what the best seat is, and hoping one day to get placed there. She takes us up to the inventory shelves where we pull down the large volumes and hope to find the registers and call numbers that we need. She evokes inventory rooms with researchers poring over the card files, clacking the wooden drawers closed. We are sitting with her in the reading room, distracted momentarily by a neighbor's cough or an archivist's ringing phone, and yet totally caught up in our quest. Farge looks over the room and laughingly compares its occupants to "galley-slaves, backs bent, hunched over and silent."

Absorbed as we are, we experience the wonder of the register when it finally comes, its look, the touch of its binding, and the feel of its paper or parchment. We struggle with handwriting difficult to decipher and are relieved when the reading is easy. We turn the pages, hoping for discovery, not just for what we planned ahead of time, but—because Arlette Farge is our guide—for the unexpected, the surprise. We rejoice when we make a find, even though the story or event itself may be sad, troubling, ghastly, baffling; even though it may oblige us to rethink our earlier understanding of our topic and restructure it.

Farge takes us beyond the setting and performance of research to reflect on the "traps" and "snares" of the archives and on the thinking we should do as we take our notes. Her specific examples are drawn from the police archives, but her counsel is relevant for people doing research in many fields, including those looking up the history of their own families. The historian must be both close to and distant from the figures, words, and events emerging from the archives. He or she must not drown in citation, or be lured into thinking that quotations will carry the story without intervention and interpretation. He or she must relish the individual or unusual case, even while seeking to understand its singularity. But her final words are for the busy worlds that emerge in reading and interpreting, always in complex movement, resisting all "abstract categories."

Newcomers to historical studies will welcome Arlette Farge's introduction to archival research. Amateur history enthusiasts will be fascinated by her insider's account of how historians practice their craft. But old-timers like me will have their memories enriched and their understanding deepened by this book. I am reminded of how much the setting for my archival research has become entwined with the discoveries I made at its tables. My first archival venture in 1952 took me to the Municipal Archives of Lyon, then housed near the Rhône in the centuries-old archbishop's palace, its dark wooden tables highly polished, its elegant lamps small and often turned off, since the war years were still close and electricity was conserved. Some days I would climb many stairs to the Departmental Archives of the

Rhône, then high above the city in the ancient convent of the Discalced Carmelites, birds serenading us from outside the windows. I still recall the kind archivist at the Municipal Archives, who helped me get started on the sixteenth-century French hand. I was surrounded by French scholars, almost all of them from Lyon itself, historians and serious antiquarians.

My most recent archival venture, in the year 2011, took me to the National Archives of the Netherlands in the Hague, in pursuit of the story of slavery in colonial Suriname. Its building dates from 1980, its fourth home since it was lodged in the Dutch Parliament in the early nineteenth century. I still take inventories off the bookshelf, but I order by computer. The very helpful manager of the delivery desk is a Dutch citizen of Indian origin; his mother is my generation. The tables and microfilm readers are filled with people from the Netherlands and elsewhere: I strike up conversations with young Dutch historians scrutinizing volumes of Dutch colonial history; Americans and Canadians on the track of figures in Dutch religious and cultural life; and people from many lands seeking their family's past. Some of the latter are from Suriname, descendants of the people of color and of the Jews and Calvinists whose wills and marriage contracts I have been reading.

One experience remains common throughout all these changes, the experience with which Arlette Farge opens her book: the direct connection with the document itself. I still recall the look of the important archival sources I've used: the large heavy volumes, with their leather thongs and sometimes their original binding; the bundles of papers tied with string, sometimes with a centuries-old pin holding pages together. In their handwriting, their occasional doodles and asides, and their registers, I have in my hands a link to persons long dead: it strengthens my historian's commitment to try to tell of the past with as much discernment, insight, and honesty as I can.

Arlette Farge's book was originally published in French in 1989, before the digitizing of books and archival records had become widespread. We had microfilm, to be sure, and many of us availed ourselves, say, of the Mormon collection of births, marriages, and deaths from many lands when we could not get to our distant archives. At the archive itself, we might be told that a document we sought was too fragile for direct consultation and available only as microfilm. The royal letters of remission that I used for my book on "pardon tales" were all read first at a microfilm machine in the Archives Nationales, but I was still able get permission to check a phrase in the great sixteenth-century parchment volumes themselves.

The current digitization of archives carries the process much further and has mixed fruits. On the one hand, there is the wonder of access, the ease with which we can bring distant documents before our eyes. Community is also possible, too, here an electronic one that replaces the exchange over lunch in the archive cafeteria or at a local seminar. On the other hand, there is the loss of the object itself, of the marginal notations missed by the camera, the signatures cut off, the paper not available to the touch, the bindings unseen. The parchment bracelets and the strange sack of seeds that Arlette Farge found among the documents are missing from the digital world. Her book is more relevant than ever in our early twenty-first century, reminding us to sustain at least some of the time our physical link with the records from the past, to read directly from the handiwork of these persons whose voices are long since stilled, and to leave our own written traces for those who will come after.

—Natalie Zemon Davis

The Allure of the Archives

Traces by the Thousands

Whether it's summer or winter, you freeze. Your hands grow stiff as you try to decipher the document, and every touch of its parchment or rag paper stains your fingers with cold dust. The writing, no matter how meticulous, how regular, is barely legible to untrained eyes. It sits before you on the reading room table, most often a worn-out looking bundle tied together with a cloth ribbon, its corners eaten away by time and rodents. It is precious (infinitely so) and damaged; you handle it cautiously out of fear that a slight tear could become definitive. You can tell at a glance whether a bundle has been opened even once since it was first stored. An intact bundle is easily recognizable. Not by its level of deterioration—after all, it may have been subjected to damp cellars and floods, wars and disasters, frosts and fires—but by a uniform layer of stiff dust that cannot be blown or brushed off, a scaly hide hardened by the years. Gently, you begin undoing the cloth ribbon that corsets it around the waist, revealing a pale line where the cloth had rested for so long.

Each judicial archive has its particular characteristics. This book deals almost exclusively with those of the eighteenth century, which are stored in the French National Archives, the Library of the Arsenal, and the National Library. My work as a historian has been founded upon these collections.[1]

The archives of the eighteenth century have little in common with the illuminated medieval manuscripts that preceded them. There is nothing decorative about them. They were simply one of the modes of civil and criminal administration under the monarchy, and time has preserved them as a trace of its passage. Like today, yet so unlike today, the police took statements and filled out logbooks. Superintendents and police inspectors sent notes and reports to their superiors. Suspects were interrogated, and witnesses gave their accounts to clerks, who then transcribed their words without any punctuation, following the custom of the time. The eighteenth-century judicial archives are simply the accumulation, loose sheet after loose sheet, of criminal complaints, trials, interrogations, case summaries, and sentencings. Crimes both large and small can be found here, as well as countless police reports and case summaries that describe in detail the population that they doggedly attempted to monitor and control. Usually these were collected and bundled together in chronological order, month by month. But every once in a while, they were bound together in registers or stacked in the gray cardboard boxes that contain criminal records, arranged by name and year. An archive presupposes an archivist, a hand that collects and classifies, and even if the judicial archives are the most "brutally" preserved of the archival and library collections—which is to say that they were mostly preserved in their raw form, unbound and without folders, collected and tied together with string like bales of hay—these documents were still in a sense readied for later use.

There was, of course, their immediate use: The eighteenth-century police needed them in order to function properly. But could anyone at the time have anticipated that more than two centuries later, a historian would decide to use these documents as witnesses once again, privileging them over the more familiar and accessible printed sources?

The judicial archive is quite different from printed documents and texts, "relations,"[2] letters, newspapers, or even autobiographies. Its material form makes it harder to grasp. It is excessive and overwhelming, like a spring tide, an avalanche, or a flood. This comparison with natural and unpredictable forces is not arbitrary. When working in the archive you will often find yourself thinking of this exploration as a dive, a submersion, perhaps even a drowning . . . you feel immersed in something vast, oceanic. This analogy to the ocean can be found in the archive itself. The archival inventories are subdivided into *fonds*,[a] the name given to collections of documents, which are grouped together either because they are similar in subject, or because they were donated by a particular individual. These numerous and ample archival *fonds*, stored in library basements, bring to mind the hulking masses of rock in the Atlantic, called *basses*, that are visible only twice a year, during the lowest tides. The technical definition of these archival *fonds* in no way detracts from their mysteriousness or their depth: "Groupings of documents, whatever their form or their format, that were compiled organically, automatically, through the activities of a person or institution, public or private, and whose preservation in the archives respects this grouping and refrains from breaking it up."[3]

Archivists and archive staff do not lose their bearings in this ocean. They talk about the archives in terms of how many kilometers they span, of thousands of linear meters of shelves. This is another form of gigantism, or maybe it's just a clever way of coming to grips with the archives, of taming them while at the same time recognizing the impossibility of ever taking full possession of them. These metric metaphors lead to a contradiction: stacked on shelves, measured in kilometers like roads, the archive seems infinite, perhaps even indecipherable. Can you read a highway, even if it is made of paper?[4]

Unsettling and colossal, the archive grabs hold of the reader. With a sudden harshness it opens onto a hidden world where rejects, wretches, and ne'er-do-wells play their parts in an unstable and living society. As soon as you begin to read, you are struck by an impression of reality that no printed text, no matter how unfamiliar, can give. Any printed document was intentionally produced for public viewing and meant to be understood by a wide audience. Printed texts seek to make an announcement and create a certain belief, to modify the state of things by advancing a particular narrative or commentary. They have been ordered and structured according to systems that are more or less easily discernable, and whatever form they might have taken, they have been brought into existence to be convincing and to change what people think. Official, fictional, polemical, and clandestine printed texts were circulated at a brisk pace during the Enlightenment, crossing social boundaries, often pursued by the royal authorities and the censorship service.[5] But whether its message was direct or masked, a printed document was charged with intention; its simplest and most obvious goal was to be read by others.

This is nothing like the judicial archives, which are the rough traces of lives that never asked to be told in the way they were, but were one day obliged to do so when confronted with the harsh reality of the police and repression. Whether they were victims, accusers, suspects, or delinquents, none of these individuals ever imagined that they would be in the situation of having to explain, file a complaint, or justify themselves in front of the unsympathetic police. Their words were recorded right after the events had transpired, and even if they were strategic at the time, they did not follow from the same mental premeditation as the printed word. People spoke of things that would have remained unsaid if a destabilizing social event had not occurred. In this sense, their words reveal things that ordinarily went unspoken. After a brief disorderly incident, these individuals suddenly needed to explain, describe, or comment on how "this" came to happen in the midst of their everyday lives, in their neighborhood or their workplace, on a street corner or inside a tenement stairwell. Characters begin to emerge out of these short sequences of events that describe an injury, a fight, or a theft. We can make out a long limping procession of baroque silhouettes whose habits and faults are suddenly brought to our attention, whose good intentions and ways of life are outlined.

The archival document is a tear in the fabric of time, an unplanned glimpse offered into an unexpected event. In it, everything is focused on a few instants in the lives of ordinary people, people who were rarely visited by history, unless they happened to form a mob and make what would later be called history. The archive was not compiled with an eye toward history. It describes, in everyday language, the derisory and the tragic in the same tone, for what was important above all for the administration was first to find out who was responsible and then to figure out how best to punish them. Questions are followed by answers, and each complaint, each deposition, is a scene that puts into words that which ordinarily would not have been thought worth discussing, much less being written down. The poor did not write, or wrote very little, about their own lives. The judicial archives are the domain of the petty crime and, rarely, of the serious felony. They deal more with small incidents than assassinations, and each page reveals details of the lives of the city's poorest inhabitants.

Archives of this type have sometimes been compared to *brèves*, the short items in newspapers that describe miscellaneous and strange news of the world. But a document from the judicial archives is not a *brève*. It was not created to surprise, titillate, or inform, but to better serve the police's constant need for surveillance and punishment. It is the accumulation of spoken words (fabricated or not, true or false, their importance is elsewhere) whose authors, constrained by the course of events, never intended to be authors. In this sense the archive forces the reader to engage with it. It captivates you, producing the sensation of having finally caught hold of the real, instead of looking through a "narrative of" or "discourse on" the real.

This gives rise to the naive but profound feeling of tearing away a veil, of crossing through the opaqueness of knowledge and, as if after a long and uncertain voyage, finally gaining access to the essence of beings and things. The archive lays things bare, and in a few crowded lines you can find not only the inaccessible but also the living. Scraps of lives dredged up from the depths wash up on shore before your eyes. Their clarity and credibility are blinding. Archival discoveries are a manna that fully justify their name: *sources*,[b] as refreshing as wellsprings.

Police interrogations and testimonies seem to accomplish something uniquely miraculous. They appear to have the ability to reattach the past to the present. When exploring these sources you can find yourself thinking that you are no longer working with the dead—although history remains first and foremost an encounter with death. The material is so vivid that it calls both for emotional engagement and for reflection. It is a rare and precious feeling to suddenly come upon so many forgotten lives, haphazard and full, juxtaposing and entangling the close with the distant, the departed.

It could be argued that the discovery of an autobiography or a private diary can have a similar effect, but there is still a significant difference. Even the most intimate personal notebook, abandoned in the corner of an attic and only discovered several centuries later, nonetheless presupposes that whoever wrote it was in some fundamental way looking for it to be discovered, in the belief that the events of his or her life called for a written record.[6] There is none of this in the archives. The witness, the neighbor, the thief, the traitor, and the rebel never wanted to leave any written record, much less the one they ended up leaving. Their words, acts, and thoughts were recorded for an altogether different reason. This changes everything, not only the content of what was written, but also the relationship we have to it, particularly our feeling of being in contact with the real. This feeling is insistent and stubborn, perhaps even invasive.

One Morning in the Library of the Arsenal

I feel cloth under my fingers, an uncommon coarse softness for hands long since accustomed to the archive's chill. I slip the cloth out from between two pieces of paper. The fabric is white and solid, covered in beautiful firm handwriting. It's a letter, the work of a prisoner in the Bastille, many years into a long sentence. He is writing his wife a pleading and affectionate letter. His dirty clothes were being sent to the laundry, and he took advantage of the occasion to sneak out a message. Nervous about the outcome, he begs the laundrywoman to please stitch a tiny blue cross on a pair of his cleaned stockings. This sign would reassure him that his cloth note reached his wife. That this piece of cloth now sits in the prison archives says of itself that no small blue cross was ever stitched into the prisoner's cleaned stockings . . .[7]

I come across a slightly swollen file, open it delicately, and find a small pouch of coarse fabric pinned to the top of a page, bulging with the outlines of objects that I cannot immediately identify. A letter from a country doctor accompanies the pouch. He is writing to the Royal Society of Medicine to report that he knows a young girl, sincere and virtuous, whose breasts discharge handfuls of seeds each month. The attached bag is the proof.

I face the decision of whether or not to open something that has not seen the light of day in two centuries. I open it delicately, withdrawing the thick pin from the two large holes it has poked in the slightly rust-stained twill. This way I will be able to close the pouch neatly by fitting the pin back into the holes, just as it was before. A few seeds escape and rain down on the yellowed document, as golden as they were on their first day, a brief burst of sunshine. What if these really came from the woman in the bloom of youth whom the doctor so trusted? Puns aside, this feeling reflects the surprising power of these seeds, still intact, as real as they are immaterial, meant to be both the fruit of a body and a scientific explanation for menstruation.[8]

These two objects discovered accidentally while consulting the documents communicate the feeling of reality better than anything else can. Not to mention the playing cards, whose backs sometimes served to scrawl calculations or note down an address, or the doodles and scribbles in the margins of case summaries, traces of a distracted clerk's daydreaming or an inspector's clumsy quill. It is as if some material traces had returned from this departed world, traces of moments that were the most private and least often expressed. Moments when people were taken by surprise, or pained, or at least feigned being so. The archive preserves these moments at random, chaotically. Each time, the person who reads, touches, or discovers them is at first struck by a feeling of certainty. The spoken word, the found object, the trace left behind become faces of the real. As if the proof of what the past was like finally lay there before you, definitive and close. As if, in unfolding the document, you gained the privilege of "touching the real." And if this is the case, what's the point of scholarly debate, why come up with new words to explain what is already there on these sheets of paper (or between them)?

These overwhelming feelings never last; they are like mirages in the desert. No matter how much the real seems to be there, visible and tangible, it reveals nothing more than its physical presence, and it is naive to believe that this is its essence. This can make the "return from the archives"[9] difficult. The physical pleasure of finding a trace of the past is succeeded by doubt mixed with the powerless feeling of not knowing what to do with it.

Yes, the cloth letter is moving, and no doubt quite a few museums would be happy to put it under glass and on display. But its importance is elsewhere. Its importance lies in the interpretation of its presence, in the search for its complex meaning, in framing its "reality" within systems of symbols—systems for which history attempts to be the grammar. The sun-colored seeds and the playing cards are at the same time everything and nothing. Everything, because they can be astonishing and defy reason. Nothing, because they are just raw traces, which on their own can draw attention only to themselves. Their story takes shape only when you ask a specific type of question of them, not when you first discover them, no matter how happy the discovery might have been. Nevertheless, you never forget the color of the seeds once you have seen them, or the words on the cloth . . .

Of course, wheat does not often pop up in the archives. Once surprise has passed, the monotony of the collected events overtakes the discoveries, and a vague weariness begins to weigh you down. It's true that no two complaints are the same, no two fights bother the neighbors in the same way, but the case summaries all have the same format, and the interrogations, at first glance, all share the same structure. The same is true of the charge sheets, the lists of witnesses, and the sentences handed down. Between one sentence of temporary banishment and another of three years in the galleys, many crooks were led away, having had only a few instants to plead guilty or to claim that they were never in the place where the sergeant arrested them.

The big volumes containing lists of delinquents and prisoners are unwieldy—you must brace them against a wooden stand to consult them—and they are laconic. Thousands of unknown names live on in their endless columns. On rare occasions the names are accompanied by scraps of information, and at first it is difficult to know what to make of them. Far from the precision found in today's equivalent registers, they offer the rough shape of a record keeping and monitoring system that was only just coming into existence. They consist of long, tiresome lists, usually written by a single clerk. Sometimes the lists are interrupted, for reasons that we will never know, and never resumed, despite titles promising long chronological spans. These problems with the condition of the judicial archives are not easily resolved, and these lists are more helpful for a quantitative history than a history of *mentalités*.[c]

According to archival lore, one veteran of the archives, striving to stave off boredom, slipped a ring on each of her fingers, just to be able to watch the light play on them as her hands flipped through these endless tall pages over and over again. She hoped by this means to keep alert when consulting these documents that, while undeniably opaque, are never silent.

More so than any text or novel, the archive collects characters. Its unusual population of men and women, whose names, when revealed, in no way lift their anonymity, can leave the reader feeling isolated. The archive imposes a startling contradiction: as it immerses and invades the reader, its vastness gives rise to a feeling of solitude. This solitude teems with so many "living" beings that it seems impossible to take them all into account, to write all their histories. Traces by the thousands . . . the dream of every researcher—think for instance of historians of antiquity. Yet while the judicial archive's abundance is seductive, at the same time it keeps the reader at arm's length.

What exactly does it mean to make use of these countless sources? How can we rescue from oblivion these lives that were never made note of even when they were alive (or if they were recognized it was only in order to punish them)? If we believed that history should be a full-fledged resurrection of the past, the task would be simply impossible. And yet, this clamoring population of the archive seems like a plea. Faced with it, you feel alone, like an individual confronting a crowd. Alone, and more than a little fascinated. You feel both the power of the contents of the archive and the impossibility of deciphering them. You realize that it is an illusion to imagine that one could ever actually reconstruct the past.

There is a tension here, even a conflict. The passion for gathering everything and reading it in full tempts us to revel in the archives' spectacular richness and limitless contents. But, logically, we know that for a document to take on meaning it must be questioned pointedly. The decision to write history from the archives comes from somewhere between passion and reason. Each vies with the other, without ever quite overwhelming or stifling its rival. They do not become one and the same, but they eventually work side by side, to the point that you are no longer conscious of the necessary distinction between them.

Imagine for a moment a document laid out on the library table, placed there by the reading room staff in the state in which it was originally compiled and organized, ready to be consulted by hand. This is by far the most common presentation; mechanical reproduction has moved forward slowly in France. Eighteenth-century manuscripts are too fragile to be photocopied, and modern technology can capture them only through the medium of microfilms or microfiches, which are sometimes necessary but hard on the eyes. Consulting a document by leafing through it, going over it backward and forward, becomes impossible with this unfeeling photographic technology, which perceptibly changes the act of reading and with it the reader's interpretation. These systems of reproduction are useful for preservation, and undoubtedly allow for new and fruitful ways of questioning the texts, but they can cause you to forget the tactile and direct approach to the material, the feel of touching traces of the past. An archival manuscript is a living document; microfilm reproduction, while sometimes unavoidable, can drain the life out of it.

Reading the archive is one thing; finding a way to hold on to it is quite another. It may surprise the uninitiated to learn that the hours spent in the library consulting the documents are often hours spent recopying them word for word. In the evening, after this strange and banal exercise is finished, you find yourself questioning the value of this industrious and obsessive activity. Is it lost time or the utopian dream that you could actually recover a time that has been lost? This task is reminiscent of childhood autumns and primary school, spent surrounded by dead leaves, recopying corrected dictations that the schoolteacher has judged inadequate the first time around. But it is also something else, something difficult to define. It lies in a gray area between the childhood process of learning to write and the mature exercise of studious Benedictines, whose lives were dedicated to the transcription of texts. In the digital age this act of copying can seem quite foolish. Maybe it is. It's true that there is certainly something foolish about always recopying the entirety of a document, instead of just taking notes or summarizing its main theme. And it would indeed be foolish, stubborn, maybe even pridefully obsessive . . . if this exact recopying of words did not feel somehow necessary, an exclusive and privileged way of entering into the world of the document, as both accomplice and outsider.

You can try reasoning with yourself, arguing that you can know Diderot very well without ever feeling the need to recopy his books. And yet, standing over an archival manuscript there is a feeling of urgency, an urgency to let the jolting current of spoken words course through your pencil, into the back and forth of questions and answers, into the anarchy of words. This flow of words can also sweep you off into unexpected directions, taking you to a place poised somewhere between the familiar and the exotic.

The allure of the archives passes through this slow and unrewarding artisanal task of recopying texts, section after section, without changing the format, the grammar, or even the punctuation. Without giving it too much thought. Thinking about it constantly. As if the hand, through this task, could make it possible for the mind to be simultaneously an accomplice and a stranger to this past time and to these men and women describing their experiences. As if the hand, by reproducing the written syllables, archaic words, and syntax of a century long past, could insert itself into that time more boldly than thoughtful notes ever could. Note taking, after all, necessarily implies prior decisions about what is important, and what is archival surplus to be left aside. The task of recopying, by contrast, comes to feel so essential that it is indistinguishable from the rest of the work. An archival document recopied by hand onto a blank page is a fragment of a past time that you have succeeded in taming. Later, you will draw out the themes and formulate interpretations. Recopying is time-consuming, it cramps your shoulder and stiffens your neck. But it is through this action that meaning is discovered.

On the
Front Door

On the front door there is a sign listing the library's hours. There is no way for the uninitiated to know that they do not necessarily coincide with the hours the documents are available for consultation. Lower down on the sign, one can find a list of holidays, as well as the accompanying days the library will be closed before and after weekends. It's a long text, unostentatiously typed on plain paper bearing the letterhead of the Ministry of Culture, posted so discreetly that one rarely notices it at first glance. Which is exactly what happens to our reader. Pushing open the heavy door, he is completely unaware that he is arriving ten minutes before the consultation of the documents ends for the morning. He is not particularly concerned; walking up from the Metro he only glanced around vaguely to spot a nearby café where he could spend his lunch break.

The building is majestic, the stone staircase is very comfortable: large, even steps tailored to the rhythm of the climb, and a smooth banister ending in a fake crystal ball that is tilted slightly to the right. On the landing there is a bust of some unknown figure, whose name engraved underneath is of no help. Our reader guesses that perhaps this was some erudite archivist, or perhaps a generous donor, and goes on his way. Large painted murals, vaguely bucolic and markedly academic, darken the walls of the adjoining hallways. There is a chill. Despite the mildness of the temperature outside, the air in here is cold and damp, and he hunches his shoulders together. In front of him are several closed doors, which seem to promise access to a reading room. But nothing indicates one door over another. It is at this moment that he begins to lose a little of his confidence. We see him hesitate, slightly intimidated, before affecting an air of false certainty. He has lost the relaxed nonchalance of his arrival, especially since he has just spotted several people whose appearance is unmistakable. They are veteran readers, their footsteps regular and quick. They inhabit this space unpreten-tiously, but with the characteristic ease of those who have long grown accustomed to this sort of warren. Someone brushes past our reader, leather briefcase in one hand, the other wrapped around a folder that at one point must have been orange. This is a lucky break. Our reader follows in the other's steps and takes on, from this moment, a more confident demeanor. He walks down a first hallway, crosses an empty space, spies the name of a room inscribed on the lintel of a door, looks distractedly out the window at the tops of the trees, and enters a vast antechamber furnished with three faded velvet benches and two display cases containing ancient medals. Through a half-open door to his right he can see down the long black rows where thousands of boxes are crammed in together, as if it were the day before a move or the day after an evacuation. He scrupulously follows the other man who courteously holds the doors for him despite the fact that his hands are full. Once he has crossed the final hallway, a gust of warm air informs him that he has now entered the reading room.

Seat number 1 is by far the best in the room. Close to the high window, it is well lit, there is no neighbor to the left and the aisle leaves plenty of space for one's elbow to roam freely. From this seat there is a nice view of the room and the narrow gallery with wooden railings that overlooks it. Each morning at ten o'clock there are at least two people who have decided that this seat will be theirs. Over time this has led

to a small war, silent, inconspicuous, but dogged. All it takes to win is to be the first to arrive in the entrance courtyard, and to make sure never to be outflanked by any movement that would allow the other, in an unguarded moment, to pass in front. No outsider can understand that this is a merciless battle, that a good seat in the archives is one of the most precious things there is. You have to start quite early to obtain the 1 seat without any difficulty and without seeming to struggle. The key is making sure not to take too long at breakfast, to buy the morning newspaper without glancing at the headlines, so that upon emerging from the Metro, eyes alert out of fear of recognizing the interloper, you can walk, without rushing, to the main entrance. If, by chance, he emerges from the same train, you must never greet him or even smile at him. Any complicity would inevitably entail troublesome compromises of principle. You must continue on your way, and then furtively take a shortcut down a small and little-known alley. If you find yourself side by side with him when the doors open, then as you walk up the stairs you must assume the detached air of someone who simply knows that the 1 seat is rightfully theirs. The enemy, faced with this beautiful self-assurance, will have to take the 2, right next to it, or better yet, the 16, directly facing the 1, and therefore well-lit, with a nice view in the opposite direction, et cetera, but especially valuable because it allows one to stare implacably at the holder of the 1. It's an unbearable confrontation for the winner, who is always a little rueful over having won so derisory a victory.

There is no détente in this competition that is waged every day. But there are also some mornings when you are wearier than others, and you concede defeat as soon as your feet hit the floor. It then becomes easy to daydream in front of a cup of tea, draw a luxurious bath while chatting with the cat, or perform three acrobatic steps in front of a half open window. The battle is lost, because at this hour the other is already sitting in the seat. You must try to view this defeat with indifference, or perhaps even carry on as if it were a new victory. It depends on how fit you feel that particular morning, and especially on whether you were able to pour your tea from the kettle without spilling any down the sides. In this case you can take as much time as you want, listen to the morning news all the way up to the weather, and stroll down the boulevard petting all of the dogs, instead of grumbling about having to avoid their messes. Stepping out of the Metro station you feel like Napoleon on the morning of the battle of Austerlitz; you have conceded the better ground to the enemy, but only so as to better defeat him. It is 10:30 and no one is left in front of the door. You will enter the reading room in triumph. The occupant of the 1 is there, tense from not having had to fight this morning. All that is needed is to brush against him a little, distractedly, your eyes lost in the lines of bookcases at the end of the room, and then walk away nonchalantly toward the other side of the room, behind him, seat number 37. A furtive glance to the side gives a view of the back of the opponent's neck, which has just tensed up imperceptibly. It's understandable, seat 37 is such a charming spot . . .

On the Front Door

Paths and Presences

To give preference to the judicial archive presupposes a choice, and presents an itinerary; to make it the sole basis of one's research or to bring it into the historical debate as one's principal interlocutor is not altogether natural. Why deny it? There's certainly something a little quaint about spending years of research obstinately parsing reports of lives led centuries ago, even as increasingly elaborate new ways of thinking about history are all the while being formulated and reformulated. But we should not forget to what extent the judicial archives themselves made many of these breakthroughs possible in the first place.

The Watchful City

Let us begin with the city, Paris, a character in itself, existing entirely in the lives of the people who are simultaneously its inhabitants and its creators. The city is molded out of their forms of sociability, which are themselves fitted to the city's tangled allure and buildings without secrets.

Flooded with people, attentive to every minor occurrence, the city is buffeted daily by the stream of news and rumors that courses through it. Sometimes hit by bad luck or accidents, the city defends itself energetically against any aggression. Naturally sensitive to the collective events that punctuate its calendar, the city prepares itself with either goodwill or indifference to the "planned jubilation" of royal festivals or fireworks. In the infinite detail of their regulations, police reports describe a city alternately anxious, feverish, or even pleading. They also portray it as devil-may-care or hot-tempered, reacting with tenacity and vigor to all that comes its way.

The city is always awake, on its guard. It uses every means to make its opinions known, whether they be good or bad, because the city is frightening. It frightens people of means and travelers; it frightens the police as much as the king. And throughout the eighteenth century it retains enough of its mystery to generate countless notes by a police force determined to let nothing escape from its shadow. Through this impressive array of material, as through Louis-Sébastien Mercier's chronicles[1] or Nicolas Rétif de la Bretonne's narratives,[2] the city shows itself to be elusive, despite an administration that seeks its submission and docility through strict surveillance. Indeed, the city is opaque and nimble, and we can discern its disorder from the monotony of regulations tirelessly repeated month after month, and rarely obeyed. The city does not listen much, and orders from on high have little hold on its light-hearted and jeering tumult. The police archives lay bare the city, usually stubborn, sometimes subdued, always somewhere else when the dream of the police is to definitively hold it still.

The judicial archives, in a sense, catch the city red-handed: craftily maneuvering around the rules, refusing outright to accept the policemen's vision of order, choosing to acclaim or snub its kings, and rising up whenever it feels threatened. When reading the police records, you can see to what extent resistance, defiance, and even open revolt are social facts to which the city is accustomed, whose first signs it quickly recognizes, and which it can instigate and direct.

The People Through Words

The archive shines a light on the people of the city and their many faces, picking out individuals from the crowd, and casting silhouettes on the city walls. The archive is born out of disorder, no matter how small; out of the darkness it snatches breathless, disjointed beings, summoned to explain themselves before the court. Beggars, quarrelers, vagrants, lechers, and thieves are suddenly pulled out of the jostling crowd, snagged by a power that has pursued them into the heart of their daily pandemonium. Perhaps they were in the wrong place at the wrong time, or they sought deliberately to transgress and offend, or maybe they wished finally to make themselves heard by the authorities.[3] The fragments of life recorded here are brief, but striking. Pressed between their few words and the violence that, all of a sudden, brought them into being for us to encounter, their presence fills documents and ledgers. The sentences handed down after a trial are often quite succinct: "hard labor in the galleys," "suspected of sedition," "sent to prison,"[4] but despite their conciseness, they reveal familiar scenes of an urban life where order and disorder were entangled before they came to be opposed, rather than some hidden criminal underworld.

Usually, the archive does not describe people in full. It cuts them out of their daily lives, cements them in some complaint or pitiful denial, and, even when they are consenting, pins them down like trembling butterflies. They remain stuck pleading, in clumsy and timid words, and

Paths and Presences

behind their apparent confidence hides the panic of a child. Unless, of course, they are operators and cajolers, or even worse, shameless swindlers and deceivers.

From the very start, the archive plays with truth as with reality. When unveiling a drama, the archival record occupies an ambiguous position in which the words of these ensnared actors contain perhaps more intensity than truth. Confessions and evasions, stonewalling and distress, are jumbled together and hard to separate. But the testimony's murkiness cannot hide the intense burst of life that shines through it. This archival shudder, truth-telling despite its possible falsity, stops us in our tracks and provokes reflection.

Of course, it is possible to imagine working only with the archival documents that are tangible and reliable. Lists of prisoners or galley slaves, for example, are indexes of isolated populations, on which you can base your research. It is altogether legitimate and important to focus your time on a particular category of delinquency—thieves or murderers, smugglers or infanticides—the study of which sheds light on the culprits as well as the society that has condemned them. Deviance and marginality are powerfully indicative of political authority and of norms, and each type of crime reflects an aspect of the society in which it occurred.

However, reading documents simply for the trustworthiness of their reporting exiles from your purview all that is not duly "truthful" or verifiable, and yet has been recorded. A few transcribed phrases, taken from interrogations or testimony, phrases that we can neither count nor classify, but which were one day spoken and assembled into a discourse—no matter how thin it may be—on which a fate was wagered. These meager discourses, true or false, given under perilous circumstances, are emotionally gripping and draw us in as readers. We must therefore look deeper, beyond their immediate meaning, and interpret them further, at the heart of the circumstances that permitted and produced them.

Throughout these discourses, lives hinged on a few phrases, and it is through these words that their speakers chanced success and risked failure. It is no longer a question of whether a narration is factually accurate, but of understanding how it came to be articulated in the way that it was. How was it shaped by the authority that compelled it to be given, the speaker's desire to convince, and his or her pattern of speech? We can then examine these words to find whether they were borrowed from cultural and rhetorical models of the time.[5]

These guarded, enduring words are at the heart of the eighteenth-century political and police institutions that governed and produced them. When examined, they offer up the stories of their origins and their existence, which were possible only within specific practices of power. From the verbal explanations given and the answers disclosed emerges a picture of the way that individual and collective behavior are interwoven, for better or for worse, with the conditions imposed by the exercise of authority. The fragile paths of these men and women, revealed in but a few words, vacillating between mediocrity and ingenuity, expose the necessary adjustments made between the individual, the social group, and authority. Of course, there are a thousand ways to answer when one is under interrogation. But any of them will reveal that the flimsy shelter one can build from words must necessarily be designed to accommodate both the existing power structures as well as the contemporary forms of explanation and description of events. These lives, neither grand nor trivial, entered history through the world of the police, where it became necessary to invent, out of fright or resignation, answers that were at times enigmatic or incisive, fruits of an unexpected moment of insertion into the social system.

These incomplete discourses, given under duress, are elements of society, and they help to characterize it. Being forced to talk in an effort to avoid prison, deciding to confess or not, hurling oneself into debate against the authorities, are marks of singular fates. Therefore, even if the discourse is muddled, mixing lies and the truth, hatred and cunning, submission and defiance, it does not diminish the "truth" that it carries. The archives do not necessarily tell the truth, but, as Michel Foucault would say, they tell *of* the truth. Namely, the unique way in which they expose the *mode of speech* of an individual, wedged between the relationships of power and herself, relationships to which she is subjected, and that she actualizes by expressing verbally. Visible here, in these sparse words, are elements of reality that produce meaning by their appearance in a given historical time. It is with the conditions of their appearance that we must work; it is here that we must try to decipher them.

Underneath the words recorded on these criminal complaints we can discern the ways in which those involved attempted to position themselves vis-à-vis the authorities that constrained them. Each individual articulated his or her own life, with varying degrees of success, with reference to a social group and in relation to the authorities. To do this, each person attempted to appropriate the dominant vocabulary, and at the same time tried, successfully or unsuccessfully, to echo that which would allow her to be found innocent—or the least guilty possible.

Beneath the archives lies an organized topography. You need only know how to read it, and to recognize that meaning can be found at the very spot where lives have involuntarily collided with authority. A sudden shock brought these situations to light, and so it requires patience to identify the dissonances and the gaps, to put the different elements in order. The reality of the archive lies not only in the clues it contains, but also in the sequences of different representations of reality. The archive always preserves an infinite number of relations to reality.

Into this complex game, in which figures appear, if only as sketches, slip fable and fabulation, and perhaps even the ability for someone to transform everything into fantasy, to write one's story or to turn one's own life into fiction. The archives also shed light on this transformation, and by locating the models that the stories borrowed from, we can discern further meaning. Narration and fiction are woven together. The resulting cloth is fine-spun, and one cannot easily spot the seams.

You could painstakingly put this all in order and meticulously examine it, but there is something else, something without a name that scientific examination cannot quite explain. Indeed, science does not feel the need to explain it, even when confronted with it. It is, of course, the surplus of life that floods the archive and provokes the reader, intensely and unconsciously. The archive is an excess of meaning, where the reader experiences beauty, amazement, and a certain affective tremor. The location will be secret, different for each person, but, in every itinerary, there will be encounters that will facilitate access to this secret place, and most of all to its expression. Michel Foucault was one such encounter, at once simple and destabilizing. He loved manuscripts and the archives, and could describe how much these sparse texts impressed him: "[It is] without a doubt one of those impressions that is called 'physical,' as if there could be any other kind."[6] Shaken, he knew that analysis could not reveal everything, but also that emotion on its own would do little to satisfy historians. Nevertheless, he did not distance himself from this way of reading documents, as legitimate as any other, although few knew him for it: "I admit that these accounts, which have suddenly leapt across two and a half centuries of silence, have resonated with something deep inside me, more than what we ordinarily call literature [. . .] if I have drawn on them it is most likely because of the resonance I feel when I encounter these small lives that have become ashes, revealed in the few sentences that cut them down."[7]

To feel the allure of the archives is to seek to extract additional meaning from the fragmented phrases found there. Emotion is another tool with which to split the rock of the past, of silence.

Her Presence

The city of Paris, its people, and then their faces leap out from the archival record. At the same time, between these handwritten lines, we clearly see one thing that was not discussed, because it seemed as if it was always being talked about: women. In the archives, apparent gender neutrality is torn away and the give-and-take of sexual differentiation is laid bare, even if the subject itself has been neglected.

The archive speaks of the Parisian woman and makes her speak. Motivated by urgency, our first step is clear: seek her out, collect her like an unknown plant or an extinct species, trace her portrait as if rectifying an omission, and exhibit her features as a body would be displayed. This is a useful task for the collector, but an incomplete one. To make women visible, when history has omitted them, implies a corollary task: to work on the relationship between the sexes, and to make this relationship the subject of historical study.

Women are astonishingly present in the eighteenth-century city: they worked, moved around, and fluidly, naturally, took part in the ensemble of urban activity. Finding them is child's play, because they constantly filled the buildings, markets, riverbanks, and fairs. Like men, they were often migrants. Arriving from the countryside, alone or accompanied, a woman would seek to establish herself and tame the city and its neighborhoods. She needed to find both lodging and work at the same time, and the archive follows her in this undertaking. It only takes an incident in the street, a theft from a market stall, a dog bite, or an upended cart to bring her into the picture through police reports and depositions. In these instances we see her navigating a social milieu that was made up as much of crowded elbowing as of effective solidarity. The archival record is sufficiently clear and rich in detail to allow us to go beyond a simple, rigid "reproduction" of her manners and dress that would freeze her in time, a motionless portrait in the style of engravings from the period. Instead, the archives, through glimpses, reveal a lively sketch of her as she lived, juggling the many uncertainties of social and political life.

The handwritten records initially tell us about the events that are often considered the most traditional: promises of marriage, girls seduced and then deserted, abandoned children, conjugal disputes, and school records. These catch her at the heart of her conflicts and desires, sometimes shaken by the violence of the times, male aggression, misery that was all too visible, or the simple pleasure of encounters that would later be regretted. But there is more to it than this. The archives find her not just caught in these circumstances, but also in motion as she sought to find fulfillment. Thanks to the archives, she is not just an isolated object, with her manners and customs on display, but a being immersed in specific ways into the social and political life of the time, immersed in the masculine world, and taking part in it every day.

This makes it possible to overcome a handicap that has somewhat hobbled the early development of "women's history," as it has come to be called. Its initial, necessary appearance in historical work and research often took the form of a supplement to what we already knew, rather than an examination of women's interactions with their surrounding world. By over-describing women, giving them a separate chapter in any well-informed thesis, we did not explain anything and gave the impression that for all intents and purposes history was happening elsewhere and in a different way. We knew about women, we knew about their lives, we described their work, their rates of reproduction, and their illnesses or misfortunes, but we did not introduce them into the action at all. In the archives, however, women are not isolated. Quite the contrary. We can spot them easily in brawls and quarrels, passing through the streets and inhabiting their buildings, laboring in workshops and market stalls. These episodes offer us the opportunity to gain a deeper understanding of masculine and feminine roles.

First of all, when called in by the police to explain themselves, women did not express themselves in the same manner as men, and they answered questions with a thought process that was fully their own. This difference may not always be visible in interrogations, where answers were strictly guided by monotonous questioning, but when they came in to file a complaint or petition, women told their pain and their disgust differently from men. However, this does not mean that they relied on methods one would traditionally imagine: you rarely encounter faint-hearted pleading, appeals to emotion, or reliance on compassion. Instead, these women, violent and defiant, preferred to speak loudly and forcefully, without falling back on their legendary frailty. Using every detail to convince, they break through the solemnity of the archival narration, rendering it more accessible and familiar, albeit quite uneven and fragmented. Their speech was often shaky and full of movement, a fast rhythmic enumeration of a sequence of unexpected events, which reveals more than just an integration into collective life. We can see the true roles that they played within the city.

Through their words, we can distinguish the distinctive and effective complicity that women established with their world. They were the spirit of their neighborhoods, passing rumors and news along a network of local personalities whose haunts and habits were always well known to them.[8] When described by women, buildings and markets come to life, becoming composed of comings and goings, travels and emigrations, and men and women busy trying to carve out a profit or a livelihood, at the risk of finding only misfortune. Women were at the forefront of these networks of neighbors and sociability that existed outside the fixed structures of the recognized trades. They were the ones who made the traditional solidarities work, but they also filled these spaces with conflicts that would later have to be smoothed over.

In the places where the archive is less disjointed, where the interrogations have yielded answers that form short narratives, allowing us to reconstitute a string of events to follow, the roles fit into place, and the give-and-take of masculine and feminine coheres before our eyes in all its complexity. Instead of being fractured by shards of descriptions picked up here and there, the female form is freed from the anonymity of the crowd, and profiled in all its ampleness. Once this has been accomplished, we can do away with a whole host of stereotypes, and the distribution of roles takes on form and agency, in ways that are at once unexpected and contradictory.

Women are visible in a variety of events, whether they were commonplace, regularly occurring, or exceptional. They can be found in full force at the port of the Seine, as

Paths and Presences

the wait grew longer and longer for their children to board the barges that would take them to faraway wet-nurses. Like the women who furtively deposited their newborns on church steps, these mothers were full of solicitude, and prepared to go to great lengths to protect their children. We see them again later (often much later, because some mothers could obtain the means to secure their children's return voyage only after one or two years), at the same port, waiting for the barge's return, and looking for their initials embroidered on a child's clothing, the only definite way to recognize their own child.

When the bailiffs and policemen in charge of seizures at unauthorized workshops dropped in, she was there, most often alone, in full negotiation and fearlessly exculpating her husband. Likewise, if she was the companion of a *chambrelan*[9] who was discovered by the police, she can be found pugnaciously defending his tools and belongings while he surreptitiously slipped off until things cooled down.

There are also women who were angry, and determined not to be swayed from their anger. In a village not far from Paris, where the houses dotted a sloping hillside, tax collectors had come to collect the money owed. They arrived on horseback, and were surprised to see that there was no smoke rising from the chimneys. The village was completely deserted, playing dead. Below a bend in the access road, the taxmen could make out a group of people through the trees; the women and children were assembled, standing stock-still, frozen in place in an effort to camouflage themselves among the trees. When called out to from afar, they replied that they were alone, and that the tax collectors should go on their way. Which they proceeded to do without hesitation, although they looked over their shoulders three or four times when they sensed they were being followed by the women, brandishing pitchforks, having silently left their children behind. Later, when night fell, they called out to their men, who were hidden in the uncleared woods higher up the hill.[10]

These women know their power, and at certain moments the archival record finds them making use of this knowledge to slip into the expected roles, in order to defend home or hearth with conviction and without shyness. And with a sense for politics. Other scenes depict them in other places and under different circumstances, more intimate ones, where they faced the last resorts of frustrated seducers. Violent aggression and forced submission were part of their daily lives, and we should not lose sight of this out of the ideological desire of these last few years to portray women as more autonomous than dependent. During this period, the male discourse about women was acerbic. The popular literature of the time abounds with deranged descriptions where women and hatred of women were one and the same.[11] From the mouths of witnesses or suspects, the archive picks up these indictments that equate women with misfortune, destruction, and even death. The archive is not simple; its contradictory readings lead the reader to a place where

Paths and Presences

systems of reciprocal compensation play out, where ambiguous attitudes are determined, where the functioning of the confrontation between masculine and feminine can be untangled. If there is a "reality" that exists in these cases, it is the plurality of ways of being and doing, where there is only the appearance of disorder. With patience, one finds feminine behaviors that were well-reasoned, which may or may not have been complicit with masculine behaviors, and whose reasoning rested, among other things, on certain means of appropriating power.

The official political landscape of the eighteenth century did not include women, but they were never far from it. The archives, once again, surprise us. In every popular expression of emotion, in groups large and small, women were on the scene and dove headfirst into the action. Not only did they incite the men to action, but they were also mixed in with the crowd, brandishing sticks and canes, and raucously defying soldiers and police. The men, in these cases, were not surprised; some even pushed the women to the front, or encouraged them to yell from the windows above. Men knew women's strength, and that the authorities customarily spared women, or at least only punished them lightly. We can also see feminine cruelty, in cases where women fiercely set upon their victims. Chroniclers of the period are inexhaustible on the subject of these morbid details, most likely attributing to women a violence they did not wish to see in themselves.[12] But there are times when the evidence is overwhelming, when many witnesses testified to some bloody act of feminine barbarity. In these cases, we must analyze, and put these acts in the context of others, those of men and those found in literature, which perhaps served as a model.[13] Or we can try to link this continually denounced feminine ferocity with the social and political system as a whole, by taking a broader view in order to identify the mechanisms of deficiencies and compensations that could give rise to rage and a taste for death among those who first give life. There are several hypotheses we could advance. Their tenacious participation in riots is one piece of evidence. Because they were active in their neighborhoods and quick to spread news, women could easily incite uprisings without really breaking out of their daily roles. And as far as their alleged enthusiasm for blood goes, once we have appropriately discounted the source of the accusation, always male, should we not try to place it in the context of the condition of impurity and uselessness associated with their menstruation? If their blood is regularly impure and flows without reason (at the time the exact role of blood in feminine reproductive activity was not well understood), was there not a kind of absolutely satisfying transgression in seeing that of their enemies flow freely in a fight?

It is through this giant maze of spoken words and uncovered actions that we can find some partial answers to our poorly formulated questions. But no such answer is definitive, because later in the same document, or in a different document, details will emerge that put into question what we had discovered earlier and events will then cohere differently.

As we glimpse what is hiding behind the recorded discourses and break down models and stereotypes in favor of diverse modes of conduct that were often unexpected—even divergent—we may be drawn far from the customary and frequently employed conceptual lens of domination and oppression. But this is no vindication of those who would disregard feminism; the archive does not overturn the basic frameworks. True, we encounter women laboring, resolute, and integrated into the political landscape. But this does not necessarily mean that they were free or emancipated in a way that would allow us to comfortably resolve the debate over the masculine and the feminine. The archive, by continually revealing more of the same, of the other and of the different, complicates the approach to these questions, highlights contradictions, and forces us to think hard about that paradoxical century, in which women came to assume economic and political responsibilities, while nonetheless being deprived of real power. It also makes it possible to draw together and compare the whole ensemble of female realities (decisions, resistance, violence, seductions) with the medical and philosophical discussions on the subject of women, which, at the time, considered her both a problem and a problematic.

Compared with the erudite discussions of the time, the archives reject any ready-made tropes and at the same time reward reflection on sexual differentiation. The Enlightenment debate over "reason" testifies to the extraordinary power relationship between men and women. Writers expounded on women's lack of reason, without ever pausing to consider that women had a rational understanding of forms of knowledge or the natural roles they played in social relationships. The French Revolution, as we know, would later resolve this problem in its own way, by excluding women from political power.

The archives bring forward details that disabuse, derail, and straightforwardly break any hope of linearity or positivism. This eruption of words and actions shatters established models, broadens the norm, displaces conventional wisdom once and for all, and often adds a certain confusion to things that had been previously considered simple. This is a godsend for women's history, because it makes the thousands of contrasting aspects of gender conflict increasingly discernable. This dynamic intensity feeds into a question, as relevant today as it was in the past: can gender difference be thought of in terms other than inequality, even if we acknowledge that there is a constantly shifting game of liberties and compensations?

Conflict

The judicial archives bring us inside a world fitful with passions and disorder. Caught in its net, the city, its people, and the women among them take on expressions that are exaggerated, even deformed, by the material that has captured them. Once we have explored the coerced nature of the intersection between speech and authority, we face the old question of how to handle sources that have been fundamentally biased by their interaction with the criminal justice system. Why not choose to take a deliberately provocative position on this, and assert that society's character manifests itself through its antagonisms and conflicts? It is more important to say this than ever, because today there is a tendency to doubt the centrality of conflict. With the boom in the history of *mentalités*, which focused on daily life and the world of the senses, historians have enthusiastically developed previously neglected themes like private life, housing, dress, nutrition, sexuality, and maternity. In the wake of a burgeoning interest in anthropology, these themes flourished all the more because they broke with the existing conventions, which had proved too rigid in their systems and ideologies. The singular and the intimate were able to break through where before the quantitative had reigned supreme. Where Marxist readings demanded rigid interpretive grids, the historian fled to the unexplored territory of cultural habits, of states of being and ways of doing. But an inconspicuous slippage began at the same time. Having become too preoccupied with drawing away from the overloaded shores of Marxism, historians failed to notice that they often left behind the universe of conflicts and tensions, of struggles and relationships of power—the universe that is the backdrop onto which behaviors, practices, and emotions must be projected. It was not that historians ignored social differences, but that they did not choose to make them engines of their arguments. And was it not perhaps the continuing subdivision and separation of the objects of study that, bit by bit, created this widening gap?

When the history of *mentalités* proved too fragmented to be effective at recapturing the intensity of social relationships, it was gradually displaced by a relatively classical event-based history, overlaid with a supposedly rejuvenated history of ideas. The great intellectual debate over popular culture has been replaced by a kind of tacit consensus around the notion of "shared cultures." But few people are now asking how these processes of sharing actually operated, or saying that maybe it is time to return to the question of how this all worked. At the very least we can say that such sharing was often quite unequal and rarely motivated by respect for others. In these processes, we can almost always glimpse one group's desire for domination over another.

Discord and confrontation lie at the heart of police records. Why not make use of this fact, and create out of rupture and disquiet a grammar with which to read the ways existences were time and again made and unmade? It is not easy to separate the history of men and women from that of social relations and antagonisms. Indeed, certain social groups only came into being through the experience of struggle. Similarly, confrontations of groups against groups, sex against sex, the people against elites, created moments that transformed the course of history and which must be analyzed. A history of relationships of power can also take into account sufferings and deceptions, illusions and hopes. History must be able to take charge of these matters, measure the poignant and reflect on the unnamable. Conflict is a space of creation, and what comes after it rarely resembles what came before it. Even when minimal or derisory, perhaps even ritualized, conflict is a rift that illuminates "elsewheres" and creates new "states of being." The historian must not only narrate a conflict, but use it as the motor of her reflection, the source of her own narrative.

At times, the archive miniaturizes the historical object. While it provides an account of the size and spread of large social movements (strikes, riots, or the incidence of begging or criminality), it also isolates, like a microscope, the expression of individual passions. In the words recorded in these documents we hear public condemnations, denunciations, hatreds, and jealousies, each playing as much of a role in this theater of reality as love and concern for others. We cannot omit any of this darkness, this taste for destruction and death that inhabits mankind. We cannot push aside this "unsociable sociability of being" where trickery, deception, and the interest of some in the subservience of others are locked in a ruthless struggle with the desire for liberty and harmony. As Claude Mettra has written, "Humanity's tragedy lies in the fundamental discord of beings with their own flesh. To write history is to draw up the report on this discord."[14] The words in the archival documents pitch between outrage and forgiveness, and through these small lives we can hear the inaudible—sometimes ignoble—sound of humanity, and catch the insistent melody of attempted happiness and hard-won dignity.

The taste for the archive is rooted in these encounters with the silhouettes of the past, be they faltering or sublime. There is an obscure beauty in so many existences barely illuminated by words, in confrontation with each other, imprisoned by their own devices as much as they were undone by their era.

She Has
Just Arrived

*She has just arrived. She is asked for a card that she does not have.
She is then told to retrace her steps to the other room, in order to
obtain a day pass. In this next room, she is asked to present a
different card, this time one she has. She takes the pass, returns to
the first room, and presents it to the reading room supervisor, who*

takes it. She waits for him to give her a place number, but he does not look up again. So she whispers to him, asking where she should sit. The supervisor, exasperated, tells her to sit wherever she pleases, except in the front row, which is reserved for consulting the most ancient manuscripts. She obeys, chooses her spot, puts down her bag, takes out a sheet of paper, and sits down. Immediately, the supervisor calls her back, causing every head in the room to look up at the same time. He asks her to give him her seat number. She comes back after a moment; it took her some time to discover where on the table the place number is written. He gives her a pink plastic square with the same number as her table on it. She returns. She knows the call number of the manuscript that she needs, but she can only get it from the gray-smocked attendant if she fills out a white form. She doesn't know where these forms are, and doesn't see anything suggesting where they might be. She looks around in silence. She spots them in a small green basket, back in the first room where she was twice asked for a card. She heads there, picks up two copies of the form, returns to her spot, and takes out a pen to fill them out. She knows that you have to deposit this form somewhere and guesses that it's the basket in the first room. It isn't the right place. She approaches a small desk, behind which sits a different man in a gray smock. He'll gladly take her white form, but where is her pink plastic square? It's a little tricky to find her table again, but after a minute she spots the pink plastic sitting on top of her papers. She takes everything, the two copies of the white form and the pink

She Has Just Arrived

plastic square, to the gray man who in turn gives her a bright blue square with the same number as the pink one. She returns to her spot where she can only think about one thing: whether, in order to leave, she'll have to find her way back through the labyrinth she's already traveled, or if it will be a whole new maze. A quick shiver down her spine reminds her that she has in fact come here to consult a manuscript.

The way her old-fashioned high heels hammer the floor, always sticking between two uneven boards, she has to be doing it on purpose. Why is it that since the archives opened she's obstinately made five fruitless trips back and forth from her table to the section where the big Encyclopédie is kept? Why can't she just choose a spot and stick to it? It's so early in the morning.

When are they going to put a rug down to muffle the sounds of footsteps? Even if it were an ugly color or low quality, everyone would be relieved.

He can't stop playing with the signet ring on his left hand. The regular scratching of fingernail against gold puts your hair on end and becomes so nerve-wracking that the sound of cars accelerating on the boulevard is a welcome relief.

Even worse is the agitated young woman who, for a whole month now, has been sitting at the same spot and flipping through the fifteen-volume collected works of a philosopher at a breakneck pace. She never slows down or speeds up, and the sound each page makes as it turns constantly interrupts your concentration. And she's still so far from being finished . . .

Today, my neighbor with the salt-and-pepper hair has a cold. He is lost in cryptic manuscripts where he probably hopes to find the philosopher's stone. He's now sniffled ten times, slowly, conscientiously. He's known for his conscientiousness, as well as for his kindness. It's pretty clear that he's not going to stop sniffling. I find myself watching his hands closely; if he would just reach into his pocket to retrieve a handkerchief, life would become easy.

Unless, of course, the reading room supervisor is seized by one of his endless whistling coughs, which cut through the air and put him in a foul mood, causing him to turn his ire on the electric lights, finding them guilty of endangering the preservation of manuscripts. The room is now dark.

The silence in the archives is more brutal than any schoolyard racket. Their cathedral-like acoustics mercilessly amplify the body's rumblings, making them aggressive and pernicious sources of anxiety. Slightly labored breathing becomes conspicuous and agonized wheezing, and a small habit (like massaging one's nose in deep concentration) turns into a monstrous tic to be dealt with urgently by psychiatric professionals. In these enclosed spaces, everything is amplified far out of proportion; the same neighbor is just as likely to become a World War I battle tank as the smiling angel in the Reims cathedral. There are certain people who work for years with a smile constantly playing at the corners of their lips. This

She Has Just Arrived

pleasant, even friendly, detail can in the end obsess even the most patient reader, who will desperately hunt for a discreet means to wipe away this smirk. In this place anything out of the ordinary (an inoffensive glass of water conspicuously sitting on the table where an American researcher has just settled in), the most minor unusual mannerism or ordinarily meaningless gesture (a neighbor nervously twiddling an ugly strand of reddish hair), takes on such importance as to become fantastical. The reading room is filled with exotic individuals who could not be described in any ethnography, or creatures devastated by insanity, assembled here to torment one single person.

She who looks and listens to this catastrophic landscape knows that her untied shoelace may obsess her neighbor to the point of taking on a monstrous, serpentine quality. A neighbor is not an enemy, but every neighbor has something intriguing about him. The choice of documents he consults, for example, leads one to a feverish curiosity about what he is working on. Unless, of course, some detail of his appearance grabs and holds one's attention. The silence of the archives is created out of looks that linger but do not see, or gazes that stare blindly. No one escapes these wandering eyes, not even the most obstinate reader, his face clouded by work. The long rows of researchers, where backs become bent and the left-handed reveal themselves, have no other way to rest from their effort. It happens without thinking, your eyes unconsciously linger on an unknown face, become fixed on a cheekbone or an undone buckle. The insistence of the stare may cause a reader's eyes to lift from the page. Eyes meet deeply and pointlessly, but without breaking contact too quickly. Looking away immediately is a response, to hold the gaze is a wager.

In the archives, whispers ripple across the surface of silence, eyes glaze over, and history is decided. Knowledge and uncertainty are ordered through an exacting ritual in which the color of the note cards, the strictness of the archivists, and the smell of the manuscripts are trail markers in this world where you are always a beginner. Beyond the absurd rules of operation, there is the archive itself. This is where our work begins.

Gathering and Handling the Documents

For some, what I've written so far might represent a naive and outmoded view of archival research. Assembling a narrative by building relationships to the documents and the people they reveal might seem today like a vestige of outdated scholarly practices. This technique appears to have no place in an intellectual period that is both more traditional—perhaps even more conservative—and less attached to descriptions of daily life. What appeal can the archives retain when others have already said everything, or almost everything, about the beauty of research for its own sake, the dialogue we carry out with the dead, and the taking into account of the anonymous and those whom history has forgotten?[1] Especially when, today, these ways of apprehending the past are met with patronizing smiles, or, at best, are learnedly reflected on by certain intellectuals as relics of historiography.

The archive's allure, nonetheless, lives on. The taste for the archives is not a fashion that will go out of style as quickly as it came in. It comes from the conviction that the preservation of the judicial records has created a space of captured speech. The goal is not for the cleverest, most driven researcher to unearth some buried treasure, but for the historian to use the archives as a vantage point from which she can bring to light new forms of knowledge that would otherwise have remained shrouded in obscurity.

The archives are not a stockpile that can be drawn from at one's convenience. They are forever incomplete, akin to Michel de Certeau's definition of knowledge as "that which endlessly modifies itself by its unforgettable incompleteness." Paradoxically, while the bundles of criminal complaints exist by the thousands and there seems to be an inexhaustible supply of words to sift through, the incompleteness of

Gathering and Handling the Documents

the archives coexists right alongside the abundance of documents. The words copied down by the clerk might give the impression that it is possible to know everything, but this is an illusion. The seeming limitlessness of the words does not entail a similar limitlessness of information. Rather, the abundance itself should convince the historian that the accumulated clues leave so much unsaid, and cause her to recognize that she is only barely capable of perceiving the reasoning of the individuals she finds immobilized in, and by, these documents. In the eighteenth century, the archives were not lacking, but they created a void and emptiness that no amount of academic study can fill. Today, to use the archives is to translate this incompleteness into a question, and this begins by combing through them.

"Combing Through the Archives"

Contact with the archives begins with simple tasks, one of which is handling the documents. Combing through the archives[d]—a beautifully evocative term—requires a host of tasks, and no matter how complex the planned intellectual investigation will be, they cannot be bypassed. They are both familiar and simple, and they purify one's thoughts, temper the spirit of sophistication, and sharpen one's curiosity. These tasks are performed without haste, and necessarily so. One cannot overstate how slow work in the archives is, and how this slowness of hands and thought can be the source of creativity. But more than inspirational, it is inescapable. The consultation of these bundles, one after another, is never finished. No matter how carefully you prepare beforehand, sampling documents and putting together research guides in an effort to limit the number of texts you will have to consult, your patience will inevitably be tested.

Reading patiently, in silence, you will regularly run up against various obstacles as your eyes travel across the manuscript pages. Many documents have deteriorated physically, and torn corners or margins nibbled away by time can swallow words whole. The writing in the margins (police inspectors and lieutenants regularly annotated documents sent to them by an observer or superintendent) has often become illegible, and a single missing word can leave their meaning in suspense. Frequently, the top and the bottom of the document have been damaged, causing entire lines to vanish. Or there will be a telltale tear at the fold and therefore an absence; many documents were removed and delivered to the lieutenant general and others.

Bad weather is a poor conservator. In the archives of the Bastille,[2] certain documents were temporarily stored in damp cellars where they absorbed the rainwater that regularly leaked in, before then being carefully reinventoried and catalogued. The ink has run, words are blotted out partially or entirely, and reading these documents can be quite tricky. The haze of time has laid down its veil. In other cases, documents will have been separated from the initial backing that kept them intact, like the posted pamphlets and insults that were torn down by an eighteenth-century police force determined not to allow any subversion to linger on the city's walls. There is a storage box at the Archives of the Arsenal that is filled with the tatters of these forbidden posters. They could be compared to flotsam, but this is too dreary a term to describe these many exuberant flights of fancy and obscene jibes. Open the storage box[3] and spread out on the table these forbidden words that were so hastily glued onto urban facades, and you begin a baroque voyage into the world of denunciation, invective, pettiness, and political ambition. These scraps of posters, torn down by censorship and worn down by time, were preserved to assist the police in hunting down the many clandestine authors scattered across the city. But today, they are in shreds, poor evidence for the prosecution.

Some of these posters were printed, painstakingly composed and decorated with engravings. But the majority of them were written by hand, in stick-like capital letters so that the handwriting couldn't be identified. There is a small throng of anonymous vengeful denunciations, bold and bitter libels, which were aimed at discrediting a neighbor, or better yet his wife, often an easier target. Written with a scratchy quill on low-quality paper and ravaged by time, these posters still manage to retain their hastiness, hatefulness, and clumsiness, as well as an improbable phonetic grammar. All, or almost all, have kept some scar from their time on the wall. When you take them into your hands, you can feel the coarseness of stone still embedded in crude and chalky glue, a tactile memory in the archive.

There are also manuscripts that are perfectly preserved and legible, but nonetheless hard to read. Although, in general, reading eighteenth-century texts is not as difficult as deciphering those from the late sixteenth or early seventeenth centuries, unexpected obstacles can still arise. For this very reason, a simple case that was classified as criminal[4] has long captivated our attention. Any reader interested in this case will find herself in a rather peculiar situation once she has the bundle in front of her. The documents, although written clearly, are unintelligible to the eye alone. The date is 1758, one year after the execution of Damiens, the would-be assassin of Louis XV. The news of this event has made the violent death of the king seem possible, and popular imagination has become fascinated by this otherwise unmentionable and ordinarily suppressed idea.[5] A domestic in a household of middling nobility, Thorin, distraught over the death of his mistress, Madame de Foncemagne, awakens haggard in the middle of the night, having heard her give him orders to fast and pray, and then assigned him to a secret mission. He assures his fellow domestics, who have not heard or seen anything, that he indeed "heard and saw" his dead mistress. Then, at that moment, he falls deaf and dumb. After his life was turned upside down on that November night in 1758, Thorin underwent lengthy

Gathering and Handling the Documents

interrogations, in writing, by judges, bishops, and doctors, whom he in turn was obliged to answer in writing.

Once Thorin revealed his secret, the case became of the highest importance: he said he had been ordered to assassinate the king, and, as proof of this monstrous order, he was now deaf and dumb. The case lasted twenty years, and Thorin remained in the royal prison of the Bastille the whole time, until his madness overcame him completely. It is a very long story, with twists and turns that are fascinating to anyone interested in the question of how public order was confronted with the collective imagination of a society whose relationship with its kings had begun to break down.

The story is not only long, but hard to decipher as well. Thorin wrote hundreds of pages over the course of twenty years of investigation and imprisonment. And he wrote as he spoke; which is to say that he did not really write, so much as he reproduced on paper the sounds that make up speech. Not the sounds of words—that would be too easy— but those that make up sentences or parts of speech. There is no punctuation, of course, but there are definitely spaces, unexpected blanks between two syllables of the same word, or disorganized reconfigurations that stray far from the beaten path of spelling.

It is thoroughly surprising and difficult to read, impossible even. Your eyes alone are not up to the task; the only way to decipher it is to pronounce it out loud, to whisper the disjointed writing. And this must be done in the hushed silence of the reading room. The experience is extravagant, not only because it breaks this silence and causes neighbors to turn their heads, but in the way that meaning appears, sound after sound, as if it were a piece of music, as if the sound gave the words their meaning. The rhythm is syncopated, the pauses are not in the appropriate places, and the elisions between words are transcribed. Nothing looks like anything, unless it is articulated, and the tongue delivers the writing from incomprehensibility: "fau il fe re direse tou levin oui une maisse pour le sarme du bougatoire jenay gamay conu votre a ta chemant juqua prisan. Je vous pri de me laisé antrepar sone de ma conaysanse" turns out to be *il faut faire dire tous les 28 une messe pour les âmes du Purgatoire, je n'ai jamais connu votre attachement jusqu'à present, je vous prie de me laisser entre personnes de ma connaisance* (every 28th of the month, one must say a mass for the souls in Purgatory, I had not known of your affection until now, I ask of you to leave me with people I know). A little further, a long confession written by Thorin requires the same treatment and only then yields its meaning: "Jamais ne pour a dir que jaye faissa pour fair de la peineamoumaître ou ames canmarad, a tendu que dé le premier moman je dis à levec de Soison que je ne croyé pas qui fus person de la moisson que sa fesoi des forbrave gen et que jeneudé jamai di dumal [. . .] Je me pansé a un crime si gran que jene vouloi dir que poremi mon ameandagé dabitere avec ste femme; le mal n'est pas si gran couche avec une fame mais un pauvre domaisse qui done dans les fame il se exposé a bien déchos" turns out to be *Jamais je ne pourrai dire que j'ai fait cela pour faire de la peine à mon maître ou à mes camarades, attendu que dès le premier moment je dis à l'évêque de Soissons que je ne croyais pas que ce fut personne de la maison que c'était des fort braves gens et que je n'en ai jamais dit du mal [. . .] Je n'ai jamais à pensé un crime si grand que je ne voulais dire que j'aurai mis mon âme en danger d'habiter avec cette femme, le mal n'est pas si grand de coucher avec une femme mais un pauvre domestique qui donne dans les femmes s'expose à bien des choses.* (I could never say that I did this to cause any harm to my master or my fellow servants, from the very first moment I told the bishop of Soissons that I didn't think it was anyone in the household, that they were very good people and that I never spoke ill of them [. . .] I could never have thought of such a terrible crime, I didn't want to tell, I must have put my soul in danger by living with this woman, the sin of sleeping with a woman is not so great but a poor domestic who gives himself to women exposes himself to many things.) In his madness, Thorin worried that God was punishing him for having loved a married woman.

This is an auditory memory in the archive, a striking reminder of the role of intonation in speech, which is so fundamental to oral literature. These pages that Thorin wrote have retained a voice, an intonation, a rhythm. They uncover an auditory culture from the past in a way few documents ever could. Thorin might have been illiterate, but his writings, in their clumsy calligraphy, transmit what no ordinary text can: the way in which they were pronounced and articulated.

With less dramatic documents as well, one always begins by deciphering, moving slowly, hands and eyes growing weary. Even at times when this is not too hard, it is never particularly easy. Procedural documents are lengthy and interrogations were required to begin with interminable juridical pronouncements; police notes are often obscure or become bogged down in meandering digressions, and except in cases of exceptional discoveries, the heart of the matter is never immediately clear. Therefore, you must read and reread, trudging forward doggedly through this bog, without a breath of fresh air unless the wind picks up. And sometimes it does, often at the moment you least expect it.

It is by reading stubbornly that the work begins to fall into place. It is impossible to say here how it must be done, only how it is that it ends up being done. There is not any standardized way to work or "work-that-must-be-done-this-way-and-not-otherwise," but only tasks that can be described flexibly, by taking some distance from the almost daily obsession of "going to the archives."

Archival research starts off slowly and steadily through banal manual tasks to which one rarely gives much thought. Nonetheless, in doing these tasks, a new object is created, a new form of knowledge takes shape, and a new "archive" emerges. As you work, you are taking the preexisting forms and readjusting them in different ways to make possible a different narration of reality. This is not a question of repetition, but of beginning anew, of dealing the cards over again. You do it almost unconsciously, going through a series of motions and gestures, interacting with the material through a joint process of contradiction and construction. Each process corresponds to a choice, which can sometimes be predictable and sometimes appear surreptitiously, as if it were imposed by the contents of the documents themselves.

The Process of Connection and Contrast

After you have read the documents, you begin culling out some among them, and by the simple acts of copying or photocopying you isolate pieces of the archive.[6] You might make your selection by collecting and assembling things that are similar, or by picking out specific items; it all depends on the subject being studied. For example, if you were planning to study a specific type of criminality or offense, you must first separate it out from other crimes inside the time period you've decided on. If, instead, you have chosen to study a larger theme (women, work, the Seine), you will first have to extract documents of all kinds that could potentially deal with the subject. Then you can go through long series of particular types of documents (police notes, criminal complaints, or guild conflicts) and pick and choose what you need, in a slightly different way, based not on category but on the presence of the theme you are looking for. Whichever technique you choose, gathering and selecting shapes the object of study through the accumulation of detail. Throughout this process you must remain aware of all the other themes that surround the one you have chosen.

On the surface, the task is simple; it consists of sifting through the archives and then gathering up a certain type of document. This series, once organized, becomes the object of research. Though they may seem simple, these tasks are your first steps away from reality, if only because they require you to classify. Purposefully focusing on a particular theme (drunkenness, theft, adultery) creates a specific viewpoint that requires explanation, because the space is necessarily reorganized by the research objective.

Often you will wind up researching one topic in order to shed light on another. You might study illegal gambling in the belief that this activity will help us understand the relationship between the police and the world of libertines, aristocracy, and finance in the eighteenth century. Or you might investigate a very specific kind of theft in the belief that it is representative of the century's preoccupations, and thus hope to deepen our understanding of poverty and misery. Or you could focus on street fights and tavern brawls to test the hypothesis that violence is one of the key elements of urban society. Or study adultery in the hopes of refining the study of relationships between men and women. Whatever the specific goal may be, for this task you are searching for the similar and the seemingly identical. Once your series has been assembled, the task is reversed; you begin to scrutinize the texts you've collected, trying to break through the similarities in order to discover discrepancies, perhaps even the unique.

Gathering

When you're collecting documents there is hardly any way to leave any material aside, because the aim of the task itself is to assemble as much pertinent information as possible within certain predetermined periods of time and space. On the other hand, when you're looking for the similar, you sometimes cannot help but to linger on the different, if only to figure out whether it's anything worth using.

Over the course of this fast-paced search you will often be surprised. An unexpected document, outside of the preselected field, can interrupt the monotonous process of collection. Gossipy, suggestive, or just different, its uniqueness provides a kind of counterweight to the series that you are in the middle of assembling. It rambles, diverges, and brings out more information than you could ever have hoped for in the usual flow of combing through the archive. These distracting documents, these breaths of fresh air, can take many forms, some cheeky, some informative, and others both at once. One project I worked on involved searching through the Y series of criminal complaints filed with the superintendent of the Petty Criminal Court (stored in the

National Archives) for everything relating to acts of violence between 1720 and 1775. The survey plan, which had been decided in advance, selected one month of complaints from each of the years being studied. Leafing through these complaints in chronological order was endless, and the violent acts they described began to turn into long lists, filling up page after page. One weary morning, between two complaints, there was a document that felt different to the touch. A tactile memory in the archive.

First, even before seeing it, I felt it; the paper was of a different type and size than the others. I paused, inter-rupting my transcription. It's a letter, a misplaced letter. I read it reflexively, out of the habit of scanning through text on faded paper, and I realized that it's a letter from one police superintendent to another.

Smiling and astonished, I read: "my dear friend. i am not cruel. if your little wife was any more so than me you would be a cuckold as of this evening because i confess to you that she gets me going in a frightening way and i don't doubt that she has the same effect on others. i'm only kidding but in seriousness i will do my best to make it to your house on time. you let me know a little late and i have more than thirty other invitations today. Goodbye. Please kiss your little wife for me, when i steal kisses from her, i only do so on the chin or on the eyes or on the cheek but you old devil you get the prime territory. one kiss, a thousand kisses on your wife's cheeks or eyes are not worth half of those you pluck from her lips. God help me, i love those lips, goodbye."[7] Stolen kisses, a letter without a date, catalogue number Y 13728. I immediately recopied this half friendly, half mischievous message. This document is unclassifiable, and yet so valuable. Later on I would reflect on whether this type of spirited missive is a cultural object or not, whether it is representative of the way people addressed each other in the libertine glow of the eighteenth century. But I had all the time in the world, and what did it matter at that moment what use this document might eventually have? What was urgent was to copy down this undated and lively letter, nestled between two very serious police matters. A mutiny in the archive.

Later, on another occasion, I was working on a project that focused exclusively on the archives of the superintendent of a very working-class neighborhood, superintendent Hugues from the neighborhood of Les Halles.[8] The plan was to study his notes and collection of criminal complaints, judicial inquiries, and sentencings in minute detail. The goal was to gain a better understanding of the phenomenon of Parisian sociability across the entire length of this man's professional career, which lasted from December 1757 to June 1788. Thirty-one years. Nothing was to be left aside, everything was to be exactingly collected and noted. Here again, I faced an infinite number of criminal complaints and exhaustion looming on the horizon.

But as this exhaustion was setting in, a little archival breeze came up unexpectedly. On the 18th of January 1766,[9] a complaint was filed about an argument in the Place des Victoires between a gentleman and a coachman, whose horse had been stabbed. We learn that Paul Lefèvre, a coachman in the Place, saw "a cabriolet harnessed to a horse, and inside the carriage sat a gentleman, who he learned was the marquis de Sade, and his servant." The coachman then stopped to let his client out, which prevented the cabriolet from continuing on its way. Words were exchanged. The marquis de Sade then stepped out of the cabriolet and "fell upon the horses with his sword, piercing one of them through the stomach."

The affair was eventually settled between the parties. The marquis de Sade—and it really was him—handed over 24 livres as "payment for the injured horse" and for the time lost while it recovered. At the bottom of the judicial document is the marquis's signature. It's truly an unexpected pleasure to suddenly run into de Sade stuck in traffic in the Place des Victoires. We are able to catch a glimpse of the daily life of this character who belongs first and foremost to literature and fantasy. In this situation the marquis acted in the way that made his reputation: gratuitous violence, a sword sunk into the belly of a defenseless horse. This insignificant account confirms so well what we have heard about the vile character of this man that I find myself almost doubting this surprising coincidence; the find is almost too perfect.

There are obviously many other examples of this kind that could be cited, documents stumbled upon accidently that lead the researcher to stray from the beaten path of combing through the archives. But documents do not have to be cheeky to have this effect. There are "quiet," ordinary documents that can lead you astray and take you far from where you had planned to go or even to understand. Perhaps this is what it is to let yourself soak up the archive; to remain sufficiently open to the forms the archive contains that you are able to notice things that were not *a priori* of interest. It might be countered that saturation is hardly a scientific method, that the word itself is troublesomely vague, and that this almost childishly naive idea could easily allow faulty interpretations to slip into the research. Of course. But I am tempted to answer with a metaphor, knowing full well that this only makes things worse: the archive is like a forest without clearings, but by inhabiting it for a long time, your eyes become accustomed to the dark, and you can make out the outlines of the trees.

Traps and Temptations

It sneaks up imperceptibly, almost without warning. You can come to have such a fondness for the documents and for the archives themselves that you forget to be wary of the traps they can lay or the risk of not keeping enough distance from them.

A whole lifetime would not be enough to read the entirety of the eighteenth-century judicial archives. But instead of being discouraging, this fact can stimulate your desire to consult them, disorder and all, perhaps even without a specific goal, out of the sheer pleasure of being astonished by the beauty of the texts and the overabundance of life brimming in so many ordinary lines. The desire to recover and recount the stories of these lives is certainly not a serious fault. Accumulating an infinite number of precise details about thousands of unknown people who have been invisible for so long can be a source of such happiness that you can begin to forget that writing history is actually a different kind of intellectual exercise, one in which fascinated recollection is just not enough. But let us be clear: even if it is not sufficient, it is at the very least the soil in which historical thinking takes root. The trap is nothing more than this: you can become absorbed by the archives to the point that you no longer know how to interrogate them.

Whatever the project is, work in the archives requires a triage, a separation of documents. The question is knowing what to take and what to leave. It is sometimes the case that because of her hypothesis a historian has already decided beforehand what she will select. This makes her unavailable, which is to say that she loses the ability to save things that may not seem immediately necessary but could, later on— you never know—turn out to be invaluable.

How can you decide between the essential and the useless, the necessary and the superfluous, a significant text and one that seems redundant? To be honest, there is no ideal way to do this, nor are there any strict rules to follow

Gathering and Handling the Documents

when one is hesitating over the selection of a particular document. The historian's approach is similar to a prowler's;[10] searching for what is buried away in the archives, looking for the trail of a person or event, while remaining attentive to that which has fled, which has gone missing, which is noticeable by its absence. Both presence and absence from the archive are signs we must interpret in order to understand how they fit into the larger landscape. When traveling this unmarked trail, you must always guard yourself against the persistent temptation to identify with the characters, the situations, and the ways of thinking and being in the documents. By "identifying," I mean the imperceptible, yet very real, way in which a historian is only drawn to things that will reinforce the working hypotheses she has settled on. Unless, of course, you have one of those amazing pieces of good luck where you discover only exactly what you were looking for and—what a lucky coincidence!—it fits exactly with your profound and initial hopes of what you would find. There are a thousand insidious ways in which you can come to identify with the object of study. It can get to the point where you no longer even recognize any difference, exception, or contradiction, except insofar as it highlights the beauty of the initial hypothesis, which you have long dreamed of establishing beyond any doubt. This blinding symbiosis with the object of study is to a certain extent inevitable, reassuring, and often invisible to the historian herself. It's inevitable, and as historians we have to admit that our choices are guided by a dialectic of reflection and contrast with ourselves. It's reassuring, because identifying with something, no matter how it happens, offers a kind of relief. But it's dangerous because this mirroring of the self stunts the imagination, inhibits the mind and stifles curiosity by confining reflection to narrow and suffocating paths. Becoming identified in this way numbs the documents and saps the understanding that can be drawn from them.

One must always remain vigilant and maintain enough watchful lucidity to safeguard against a lack of distance. This type of "asceticism" does not prohibit the exchange between reader and archive, or empathy for that matter. But exchange is neither a fusion nor an abolition of differences. Rather, it is the necessary acknowledgment of the strangeness and the familiarity of the other, without which there can be no informative or effective inquiry. And this exchange requires confrontation, because quite often the material resists, presenting the reader with a face that is enigmatic, at times even cryptic. When research runs into the opaqueness of the documents, and the documents no longer readily offer up the clarity and convenience of an easy "it's like this, because that's what's written," then our work as historians truly begins. We must start with what the texts harbor that is improbable and incoherent, but also irreducible to any readily available interpretations. When the opposite is true, and the archive seems to effortlessly yield exactly what we expected to find, our work is even more demanding. A historian must painstakingly free herself from an innate "sympathy" with the archives, and instead see the documents as adversaries she must do battle with, scraps of knowledge that are unsettling and cannot be neatly squared away. It is not easy to rid yourself of an excessive ease in finding meaning in the archives. To be able to truly understand a document, one must first put aside what one has learned about it and stop believing that it could deciphered in the very first reading.

Documents can be very talkative. Sometimes, on a particular theme, they can offer up to the reader an endless supply of new information that is both judicious and detailed. When a document is this dynamic, it can give the impression that it is sufficient in and of itself. In these cases, it can be tempting to skip taking a step back from the document and go straight to commenting upon it, as if its presentation of the evidence did not need to be reinterrogated. The result is historical writing that is flat and descriptive, unable to give anything besides a reflection—perhaps even just a tracing—of what was written two hundred years ago. The historical narrative becomes a tedious gloss, a positivist commentary in which the conclusions offered have not been screened critically.

Quotations can often come to the writer's aid. But here again, you must think about the way they are used, so that they do not become a crutch or a misleading means of substituting facts where reasoning is necessary. A quotation is never proof, and any historian knows that it is almost always possible to come up with a quotation that contradicts the one she has chosen. The quotation has so much charm that it can be difficult to resist. It is charming because it is different; it has the charm of aptness and exoticism, with the colorfulness of language from another era, and even the charm of self-avowal. But to quote is to implicitly admit that you cannot find better words or more pertinent ways of phrasing things than those already in the archive. Or, you might quote in an attempt to camouflage your own inability to analyze any further, hiding behind the appearance of plausibility, even truthfulness, that a quotation can confer.

In fact, the proper usage of quotations is similar to the inlaying of precious stones. A quotation only truly takes on meaning and significance if it fills a role that nothing else could. The quotation has three principal functions. It can effectively introduce a new situation by the sheer abrupt force of its expression. In these cases, it works as a jolt to help push the story forward. Alternately, if the goal is to astonish the reader, a quotation can leap out unexpectedly, changing the focus and breaking through the predictable. This is the quotation as a rupture, which allows the historian to pivot away from herself, to rid herself of her learned academic habit of displaying the successes and failures of others. When used in this manner, the quotation interrupts the narrative. The words between quotation marks remind us that we cannot actually remove ourselves from the universe of words in which human experience takes shape. And, of course, there is another function, less lofty and certainly somewhat lazier. A quote can give some respite from the tension of a text, providing a pause, even an intermission. Not because it simply adds text on top of text, or because it shows how "well" people said things back then, but because it can modulate the writing of the narrative with bursts of images, surprising the reader with the sudden appearance of other voices. Inside the text, the quote works as a stop. Like a rest in music, it allows the historian's practiced and reasoned words to work differently around it. At the end of a sentence, paragraph, or chapter, it can build a silence around the suddenness of its appearance. This is as it should be. History is never the simple repetition of archival content, but a pulling away from it, in which we never stop asking how and why these words came to wash ashore on the manuscript page. One must put the archive aside for a while, in order to better think on one's own terms, and later draw everything together. If you have a taste for the archives, you feel a need for these alternating tasks of exclusion and reintegration of documents and writing, as you add your own style to the thoughts that emerge.

Being swallowed whole or over-identifying, producing mimicry or flavorless gloss, these are only some of the many traps laid by the archive. But there is another kind of lure, this one coming from our contemporaries both near and far.

There is no doubt that the archive contains an abundance of stories and anecdotes, and that people enjoy hearing them. In the pages of these documents, thousands of fates crossed or missed each other, presenting us with a multitude of characters who have the makings of heroes or of forgotten Don Quixotes. Even the adventures of the more ordinary characters in the archives still have a tinge of exoticism. For some, there is a novel to be written here. For others, fiction is the ideal way to free oneself from the constraints of the discipline and make the archive live again.

Although it is often evoked, this possibility is actually neither trap nor temptation. The argument that the novel resurrects the archive and gives it life is, in fact, not a real argument at all. The novelist creates a work of fiction; this is true whether or not the backdrop is "historical" or the characters were plucked from past centuries. It's true that a writer can make marionettes out of eighteenth-century men and women, adroitly or clumsily, bringing the readers in on the trick and providing entertainment. But this has nothing to do with "writing history." And while knowledge of the archives is absolutely necessary for ensuring the authenticity of the drama, the life the novelist breathes into her protagonists is a personal creation, where dream and imagination are joined together with a gift for writing to captivate readers and take them on a very specific adventure.

Lives are not novels, and for those who have chosen to write history from the archives, the stakes are not fictional.

How to explain—without seeming to brag and without disdain for historical fiction—that if we are to do right by these many forgotten lives, lives ground down by the political and judicial systems, we can only do so through the writing of history? When the prisoner in the Bastille, locked up for hawking pamphlets, writes to his wife on a piece of cloth he has torn from his shirt and begs the laundry woman not to ignore this cry of hope, a writer of history cannot turn him into the hero of a novel. It would be a kind of betrayal, if only because he would be immediately lumped in with so many other heroes, whose defining trait is that they were put in motion and controlled by an author's hand.

The prisoner of the Bastille, whose unique traces rest in the archives, is an autonomous subject, not the fruit of someone's imagination. His existence, if it is to take on weight and meaning, must not be turned into a novel; rather, it needs a narrative that is able to see him as a historical subject, a member of the society that gave him his words and expressions. If he is to "come alive," it will not be through a fable, but through writing that illuminates the circumstances of his appearance in the archives and takes into account whatever remains obscure about his existence, getting as close as possible to that which will always be missing. Unique and autonomous (despite the constraints of authority), this prisoner in the Bastille, a fugitive passing through the archive, was a person with his own reasons, put into words through the archive, whom history must take on as an interlocutor.

However much we denounce the archive's traps or the temptations it gives rise to, we must not fool ourselves. A passion for the archives is not an exemption from its pitfalls. It would be prideful to imagine that by virtue of having spotted the traps we have eluded their grasp.

Captured Speech

The judicial archives reveal a fragmented world. The majority of police interrogations consist of questions whose answers are incomplete and imprecise, quick snippets of speech and life whose connecting thread is difficult to make out.

On the other hand, the more one becomes interested in the archives, the more expressive these trivial complaints about trivial matters become—people quarreling over stolen tools, for example, or over some dirty water splashed on their clothes. Because they led to police reports and interrogations, these signs of minor disorder have left behind a trail. These personal matters where almost nothing was said, but so much transpired, are fertile ground for historical investigation and research.

The events are mundane, their occurrence beyond commonplace. The characters involved are entirely ordinary, and the documentary record of them is fragmentary. But in these tatters of lives and scraps of disputes, found here in bulk, we can find both human defiance and human misery. It is almost impossible to impose any classifications on this jumble of complaints that exudes an everyday banality. This could be an excuse to leave them aside in order to focus on something else, the history of legal procedures, or the great trials that were carried out according to correct procedure. Or we could figure out how to seize these flashes of life, intense and contradictory, sometimes violent and always complex, to draw from them as much meaning as possible.

From the Event to History
If we choose this path, and insist on working with the minute, the unique, the almost invisible, we must take care to

discuss the problems that will arise and, even before that, we must suggest an explanation of how events become history.

The words spoken, the short narratives recorded by the clerks, and the makeshift explanations stammered by suspects and witnesses are all events. These truncated discourses, which were proffered despite fear, shame, and lies, and which were attempts by the individuals interrogated to seek refuge in coherent narratives, are events. Thanks to them, we can see the specific ways social identities were expressed through representations of self and of others. They illustrate forms of sociability and ways of viewing the familiar and the strange, the tolerable and the unacceptable. The answers to the superintendent's questions were almost always vague and imprecise, sometimes intentionally and sometimes not. But under interrogation, each individual expressed herself through the images that she carried of herself, her family, and her neighbors. More than that, she tried to exert influence, without exactly weighing the power of her words. Her words are also "events," because they exist for the purpose of being believed, and it is impossible to forget this fundamental character of social interaction. These words depict an organized (or fractured) world, but they were also uttered to be as convincing as possible to those who were listening and judging. The event exists in the tight relationship between the spoken word and the desire to craft a plausible story. During some interrogations—whether because of the personality of the individual interrogated or despite it—the answers not only reveal the expected information, but open on an entire horizon that we must seek to understand. Words carry their present with them, and they tell us of the way things were recognized and differentiated. For example, when a peddler suspected of theft is asked what year he was born and replies, "[he] does not know the year, but only that he will be seventeen next St. Charles day," it would be a shame if all that we noted under "age" was "17 years old." It would take away everything that immerses this piece of information in a universe that is both personal and collective. This kind of response is not uncommon. It is part of the typical, everyday information found in the archive, which makes it both valuable and difficult to interpret. In the same way, when a man being interrogated about his family situation is asked if he has a wife and children, and answers, "no, he is a widower and his children are dead," this remark gives a quick glimpse into one man's entire world. Or even—one could list endless examples—the seventeen-year-old with twenty-one brothers and sisters, who does not know his oldest brother's name and could not identify any of his little sisters except the youngest. This fragmented expression of being is also an event, given to us as a clue, forgotten but still ringing with the echoes of the world that surrounded it.

Details of work situations provide the same type of narrative, giving us both information and that which enables us to access it, or rather that which makes it coherent. When a needle-maker is asked on what date he had arrived in Paris, he reveals the full context of his migration in a single sentence: "said that he came to Paris three years ago because he thought that he would be able to earn a better living as so many others had, but in Paris he contracted cataracts in his eye that he was not able to cure, and therefore had to give up his trade." The event is not that he is a migrant who has arrived in the last three years, but all that he has lost during this time: hope, health, job. It's also in this image of Paris as a mirage. It's the sad end of this individual dream, which was a collective dream as well, for so many migrants came to cities only to have their hopes crushed.

These responses are interesting in themselves, but they are much more than that; they can shed light on matters that range from the trivial to the essential. They allow us to glimpse the structures of social networks and the many ways people lived among others. One seemingly banal example can illustrate this better than any long explanation. A young washerwoman, accused of having taken part in seditious activities, is asked whether she has a nickname. Her brusque answer is typical. Although it may seem insignificant, her answer allows us to hear the traditional styles of popular discourse. "Are you the one they call 'pockmarked fatty'?" she replies that "[she] is not pockmarked at all, and that while it is true that for a little while now, in bantering, she has been called fat, she is not fat at all, and that often she does not even respond to this joke, because it's not her name."[1]

This "form of talk,"[2] innocuous enough, is an event because it is language as actions, as a set of behaviors. It testifies to customary practices of interpersonal interaction. Here, in a few words, we can discern a style of communication between two individuals of the same social milieu. In this interaction we can see the common practice of referring to others using mocking nicknames, as well as traditional strategies of teasing, irony about physical appearance, and an individual's insistence on only replying to her real name, the sole designation she considers appropriate. The language used in these answers expresses, with acuteness or clumsiness, conviction or fear, the complexity of social relations and the ways in which individuals tried to maintain their dignity within the constraints of the social and political world of the city.

These are all events because they reflect (albeit with differing degrees of clarity) everyday styles of communication. The language used was informed by particular cultures and competences specific to each individual. "Does not know how to read or write, he only went to school for a short while because he was told that he would learn better when he was older and that there was a teacher coming to tutor him"; "that he only knew his mark"; "when asked how to spell his name he answered that he did not know, because he does not know how to write, can only read printed writing, and in the past he has always made a cross on documents he was told to sign." These are a few answers among many, and they describe specific forms of knowledge that had nothing to do with those of the dominant culture, each representing one of the infinite ways in which written culture was apprehended and information was acquired. One might know how to read but not to write, or to write only in block letters, or be dumbfounded by capital letters, or know just a few letters and only be able to sign with a cross. These competencies are neither illiteracy nor mastery, they cannot be counted or represented on a graph, and yet these individual configurations are precious clues to the ways in which people maintained a piecemeal grasp on cultural tools. None of this is quantifiable and it is therefore impossible to specify an exact rate of illiteracy or level of education. Still, it allows us to challenge the traditional classifications and penetrate into the dense undergrowth with its infinite offshoots of knowledge from which individuals cobbled together their identities and opinions, piece by piece.

Words are windows; they will let you catch a glimpse of one or several contexts. But words can also be tangled and contradictory. They can articulate inconsistencies whose meaning is far from clear. Just when you think you have finally discovered the framework underlying the way events unfolded and individuals acted, opaqueness and contradiction begin to creep in. Incongruous spaces emerge with no apparent connection to the landscape that seemed to be taking shape only a few documents earlier.

These discordant spaces and gaps harbor events as well, and the hesitant and unfamiliar words used to describe them create a new object. These words reveal existences or stories that are irreducible to any typology or attempt at synthesis, and do not fit neatly into any easily described historical context. Although they are almost incomprehensible and resistant to any analysis, these words must be "taken hold of" because they allow the historian to capture moments of extreme tension at the very heart of society.

It is fruitless to search through the archives for something, anything, that could reconcile these opposites. Because the historical event also resides in this torrent of singularities, which are as contradictory as they are subtle, sometimes even overwhelming. History is not a balanced narrative of the results of opposing moves. It is a way of taking in hand and grasping the true harshness of reality, which we can glimpse through the collision of conflicting logics.

Fragments of Ethics

Here in the archives, conflicts predominate. Large or small, of private concern or threatening to the public order, these conflicts never follow the paths of perfectly linear narratives. These stories usually had to be dragged out of the prudently mute protagonists, who nonetheless almost always talked in the end, compelled and provoked by policemen anxious to know the facts, obtain confessions, and find the culprits.

Reconstructing the facts *a posteriori* is never easy, not least because most of the dossiers ultimately put forward only one version of the events, that of public order and police authority. The questions that were asked have a policeman's directness. Above all, the police were looking to indentify the culprits; it mattered little to them whether in the end an affair was ever fully cleared up. If, for example, there was a quarrel in the market or an uprising against some soldiers, the police arrived on the scene and made no secret of their intentions. They immediately sought out the ringleaders and toughs whom they seemed to know already and they operated without hesitation in rough neighborhoods with which they were all too familiar. Whatever the specific facts of the case may be, the police reasoned, it would give them the opportunity to clean up and impose some order on public spaces. If two women were arguing at a market stall about overpriced vegetables or fish, as soon as the police arrived they would head straight toward the suspicious market crowd of dealers, crooks, and small-time forgers. Similarly, if artisans went on strike, it always resulted in the imprisonment of a few colleagues already well known to the police for their subversive activities.

An initial reading of the documents often provides only the policeman's view of order and disorder, sometimes leaving aside the actual actors in the conflict, who generally operated on their own, without relying on the criminal underworld or on accomplices. It was always simpler for the police to go to the usual suspects, to those who always seemed to turn up whenever there was trouble.

As historians, we must take into account the reflexes, habits, and weaknesses of the police. On the other hand, we must not forget how cunning the accused could be, as they proclaimed their innocence in answers that are as outraged as they are feigned: "he wouldn't know anything about that," "he was not at all where it was alleged he was," "she didn't see or hear anything besides the sound of a commotion." These clumsy denials and artless evasions might look like little more than confessions or admissions of powerlessness. But this is only on the surface, because between the lines of these vague statements are scattered short sequences of lives, unexpected gestures, and even the shadow of the social world. To illustrate this, here are a few of these seemingly routine answers, given in response to the question that began every interrogation: "he [or she] is asked why he [or she] was arrested."

> "he doesn't know anything about any of this, he had just finished making the sign of the cross after passing in front of a doorway where there was a dead body when . . ."
> "she was busy setting up the awning of her stall, as she did every day, at the moment when . . ."
> "she had just told her son to fetch the salve for her husband's wounded leg and that . . ."

Captured Speech

"he was used to drinking a pinch of brandy at the tavern and not having to be wary of others when . . ."

"he had his good name and feared no one but God . . ."

"he heard a noise and saw that the stairwell was full of people but he continued to put away his tools . . ."

"she wasn't looking at anyone as she carried her bonnets to the laundry on Roi-de-Sicile Street when she felt . . ."

"he ran to the workshop to warn his friend about what was happening in the neighborhood, then he stayed with him a while, bantering with the serving girl from across the street who was hailing down clients, before . . ."

"she heard it said that he made the women yell out the window and she knew him to be . . ."

"she did not know the woman who stands every day near the milestone selling her lettuce . . ."

"he ordered her to run away when he heard the police coming, but that she didn't want to . . ."

"she has four young children and her husband hasn't been home in three days, and she's sure he sold everything right down to the shirt off his back . . ."

"she makes her money by doing laundry and she intends to dispose of it as she wishes, that naturally she needs money to live, and that she has a soul to save . . ."

"he attacked her with the pruning knife and the neighbors rushed in to intervene before he killed her . . ."

"he has caused him so much pain that he will only die
by his hands . . ."
"no one told him that you weren't supposed to walk at
night near the city gates and that his sister always
goes there with her friend. . . ."

Sometimes the answers are more detailed. When discussing
riots, for example, suspects and witnesses were more comfortable describing what they observed, whether it was the looting
of a bakery or a manhunt. In the rush of so many testimonies,
we can catch actions as they happened, representations as
they were crafted before dissolving away. At these key
moments of flux, nothing had been fixed in place and no
general interpretation of the event had yet been settled upon.

Each person testifies to what he saw, and to the unique
way in which he was brought into the action and improvised
his role—sometimes passionately, sometimes reluctantly,
depending on the case—in some cases even undertaking
actions that would alter the course of events. Even when
multiplied, these testimonies do not fully reconstruct the
affair in question, but they do draw our attention to the
impromptu organization of these small and furtive scenes,
the details of the actions taken, the ethical stances that were
expressed,[3] and the creative ways in which individuals
acknowledged each other.

Whether the testimonies are precise or opaque, chatty or
terse, the historian can draw much more from them than

simple details for use in reconstructing the facts of the matter. They are fragments of ethics. Fragments of ethics, in the sense that the stream of words each person used to describe herself and the events reflects an ethos, an aesthetic, a style, an imagination, and the personal link that connected the individual to the community. In the murmurs of thousands of words and expressions, you might be tempted to look only for the extraordinary or the clearly revealing. This is a mistake. Seemingly insignificant and unimportant details can reveal what was unspoken and outline lively forms of intelligence and reasoned understandings, interwoven with broken dreams and spent desires. These words trace intimate outlines and capture the thousands of ways each person has of communicating with the world.

The Accidental and the Singular, the Unique and the Collective

Singularity is disconcerting; what can be done with these countless individuals, their tenuous plans, their many disjointed movements? A single morning spent in the archives combing through a handful of criminal complaints will bring you almost face to face with some peculiar characters. The first might be a pickpocket, locked up in the Bicêtre prison and yearning for freedom who writes, "I've gotten scurvy twice now and I painfully conclude that if I remain in the Bicêtre much longer I will pass into the next world, from which it would be difficult for me to send you any news."[4] Next there is a beggar who disguised himself as a monk "carrying a box of curiosities that he had bought and that contained one *Ecce homo* and 4 depictions of the Passion that he showed to passers by."[5] Then a mother tearfully accompanying her arrested son, "holding his hand."[6] . . . Over time, hundreds of these silhouettes will pass before you, one by one.

This constant emergence of the singular invites reflection on "the unique" and on the historical concept of the individual.[7] It spurs the historian to attempt an articulation of the complex link between the people anonymously submerged in history and the society that they belonged to.

Relying entirely on anecdotes accomplishes little, however, because it does not seek to explain anything. A taste for the strange is no better, because it deforms the way we look at the documents. What is left, at the level of the spoken words, is to set about the delicate analysis of the unusual, separating it from both the mundane and the exceptional. Our task is to find a language that can integrate singular moments into a narrative capable of reproducing their roughness, while underlining both their irreducibility and their affinity with other representations. We need a language that is capable of reconstructing and deconstructing, playing with the similar as with the different. The human being captured in documents is, as Michel Foucault has written, "interwoven in his own being with histories that are neither subordinate to him nor homogenous with him."[8]

He should not simply be measured against the yardstick of the average person from his time, about whom we have little to say. Rather, these individuals should be approached with an eye toward drawing out the sequence of strategies that each person uses to make his way in the world.

If we aim to "defend stories"[9] and bring them into history, we must commit ourselves to demonstrating in a compelling manner the ways in which each individual constructed her own agency out of what history and society put at her disposal. When examined in this way, interrogations and testimonies shed light on the spaces where an individual entered into both peaceful and tumultuous relationships with different social groups, while at the same time struggling to preserve her freedoms and defend her autonomy. The history of individuals can shake our received wisdom about the ensemble of behaviors and events that we consider to be collective. Yet at the same time, we can only study individuals through their interactions with social groups.

This focus on the singular requires understanding the adjustments each person made with others, and must draw on sources besides the documents in which that person appears. It is rooted in the willingness to read, today as much as ever, about the countless ways individuals distanced themselves from the norm, about the complexity of the paths each person mapped out for herself in the effort to retain the ability to decide her own actions, so that she could belong to society but not be subjugated by it. Here is a vision of the world, an ontology of the real, an anxious determination never to let anything become rigidified. As if the words of today hold as much hope as those of the past, the hope that they might bring new possibilities.

Meaning and Truthfulness

In the end, there is no such thing as a simple story, or even a settled story. If the archive is to serve as an effective social observatory, it will only do so through the scattered details that have broken through, and which form a gap-riddled puzzle of obscure events. You develop your reading of the archives through ruptures and dispersion, and must mold questions out of stutters and silences. It is like a kaleidoscope revolving before your eyes. Pausing for an instant, it fixes the precise shapes of imagined figures, which then burst into iridescent light before coming together in different configurations. These figures are ephemeral, and the smallest movement scatters them to produce others. The meaning that can be found in the archive has both the strength and the evanescence of these images that are one by one brought forward by the whirlwind of the kaleidoscope.

The past has no unambiguous meaning, and nowhere is this clearer than in the archives. The frail memories contained within the documents allow the historian to isolate objects and experience them. "When the historian explores a subject," Jacques Revel writes, "he must build the history that he needs and do so making use of other disciplines."[10] And, as Edward Carr points out, no document can find meaning in itself: "No document can tell us more than what its author thought—what he thought had happened, what he thought ought to happen or would happen, or perhaps only what he wanted others to think that he thought, or even only what he himself thought he thought. None of this means anything until the historian has got to work on it and deciphered it. The facts, whether found in documents or not, have still to be processed by the historian before he can make any use of them: the use he makes of them is, if I may put it that way, the processing process."[11]

The desire to understand is a demanding one, and there are as many illusions to tear down as there are requirements to fulfill. The historian cannot be narrator alone; he must also explain and persuade, providing detailed explanations because he knows that contrary ones can be always be advanced. The first illusion that must be cast aside is that of the definitive truthful narrative. A historical narrative is a construction, not a truthful discourse that can be verified on all of its points. This narrative must combine scholarship with arguments that can introduce the criteria of truthfulness and plausibility. The poet creates, the historian argues. He rearticulates past systems of relationships through the representation of the social community he studies, and through his own system of values and norms. History's goal is the understanding of a time and a world. This is achieved by establishing plausible continuities and discontinuities within the past, and these are only convincing if they are grounded in academic rigor. The historian is not a writer of fables, which is why he can say, as Michel Foucault did: "I am fully aware that I have never written anything other than fictions," before adding immediately, "But I believe that it is possible to make fictions function within truth."[12]

It is possible to cast aside the illusion of universality, of a total and definitive truth that can be reconstructed in its entirety. At the same time, one cannot dismiss the truth, nor even be scornful of it. The truth must never be led astray, and the space between these two poles is often quite narrow. When building a relationship with the archive you become very conscious of these two imperatives, and of how important it is for them to work together. As a counterweight to theoretical and abstract constructions, the archive sets the mass of all the minute yet unavoidable existences and events, goading traditional knowledge with a mundane and flagrant "reality." The archive offers up faces and pains, emotions and the authorities created to control them. Being familiar with these things is indispensible to any attempt at describing the architecture of past societies. In the end, the archive will always trip up the historian who tries to escape with too much ease into the study of abstract formulations and "discourses on."

The archive is a vantage point from which the symbolic and intellectual constructions of the past can be rearranged.

It is a matrix that does not articulate "the" truth, but rather produces, through recognition as much as through disorientation, the elements necessary to ground a discourse of truth telling that refuses lies. Neither more nor less real than other sources, the archival documents display the fates of men and women whose surprising and somber actions crossed paths with an authority that had many faces. The emergence of these lives that collided with the established systems of power deserves a historical narrative that is commensurate with this outpouring and its significance. We must take into account the rags of realities that have been laid bare before us, beginning by digging beneath the unspoken to uncover the strategies of individuals and social groups, then putting these in order, and advancing a new understanding on which we can then base our analyses.

It is critical from the outset to explain the rationale behind the frameworks through which you will analyze the material. Your explanation of why you questioned the archives in the particular way that you did must be clear if the conclusions of your research are to be convincing rather than doubtful. The archives can always be twisted into saying anything, everything and its opposite. Therefore, one of the very first obligations a historian has is to clarify the manner in which she will interrogate the documents. To get straight to the point: it is one thing to understand history as a process of permanent reinterpretation of the past from the standpoint of contemporary society and its needs. It is quite another to press events from the past into the service of ideology. There are times when it is necessary to put forward indisputable "plural" truths (and not "the" truth), multiple reflections of reality that should be neither hidden nor subverted. But there are also times where history must make certain errors clear and offer proof, so that, as Pierre Vidal-Naquet put it, "memory is not assassinated."[13] "History is endlessly incomplete [. . .] but does it not remain essential to hold on to that old thing, 'the real,' that which actually happened?"[14]

As Paul Ricœur said recently during a colloquium with historians, "One must never dull the sheer force of what happened, the sheer force of the events."[15] This is especially true when these events are still traumatic. There are horrific events whose transmission is vital and whose narrative has a special status, even more so when these events live on in "cultural memory." Auschwitz, he emphasized, was a "negative foundational event," an event that we must never forget and whose transmission we must never allow to be distorted. Of course, "history is not a tracing of the real, it requires the establishing of relationships between different elements of the real,"[16] an operation that must be carried out under a strict standard of truthfulness. This is pertinent to the analysis of all historical events, but the relationship of history to reality becomes crucial in the case of facts that have become part of a living memory that reaches across our entire society.

Therefore, we cannot tolerate the "revisionist history" of Robert Faurisson and others like him, which took on new forms as it infiltrated itself more or less everywhere, insinuating that the gas chambers never existed. It is the pernicious discourse of a murderer's apologist, whose goal is to "deny the reality of the suffering, of the death."[17]

The French Revolution was also a foundational event, although a positive one, and its presence is felt up to the present day. Because this episode is still active in the collective memory, historians tend to have a very complex relationship to it. Some, for example, try to show that the terroristic and bloody Revolution was one of the most shameful episodes of our history, and do not hesitate to use the word "genocide" when talking about the civil war in the Vendée. There is no way around it, this is a manipulation of the truth. Twisting the facts, these authors have allowed passion to trump academic rigor. When subjected to treatments like these, knowledge is broken and dies. As Paul Ricœur has argued, the very sense of self is imperiled if you refuse to "live in the text of another."

Take the example of the Vendée between 1793 and 1797. The best study of this period is Jean-Clément Martin's *La Vendée et la France* (Le Seuil, 1987). He started over from the beginning, not only gathering together all of the facts and numbers, but also advancing a convincing interpretation of why events unfolded as they did. He shows to what extent the beginnings of this insurrection in the Vendée traumatized the members of the revolutionary government, who saw it as a negation of all their efforts. Out of this shock came pitiless repression, which unified a region that up until then had not known its own power. Martin poured all of his intellect, backed by the archives, into showing that facts are nothing if they are not reinserted into the way they were represented at the time, representations that can magnify them, or can diminish their development and impact. The war in the Vendée occurred at the heart of a self-reinforcing spiral of events and how these were perceived. If the revolutionary government had not seen these events as being so symbolically charged, no doubt the course of the civil war would not have been so bloody. Martin beautifully balances a factual approach to what actually happened with an understanding of the meaning that was given to these events as they spread through a succession of echoes, ricocheting back and forth, each constantly amplifying the others.

It is important to understand that outside of certain rare exceptions, archival documents cannot be definitive proof. But they are reference points we cannot ignore, whose meaning must be constructed through rigorous and precise questioning. As historians we must recognize that "the validity of the knowledge depends on the validity of the purpose,"[18] and that we must carefully navigate between recognizing the influence of our choices and the impossible theory of history as an objective compilation of facts.

Even after these precautions have been taken, the meaning you are searching for will not be lying there like a treasure waiting to be found. You must root for it beneath the apparent disorder of the narratives, facts, and events contained in the archives. For example, if you are studying popular behavior, you must track down the full-fledged systems of reasoning that caused the social actors present in the documents to speak and act in the ways they did.

Understanding Certain Forms of Popular Expression

There is always a risk that a history of popular behavior based in the archives will become reified. This is especially true if you do not look past the details you have gathered on social practices, both emotional and political, to reach the modes of thought, autonomous behaviors, and systems of reasoning that underlay them. Our work is not finished once we have described a population's attitudes and behaviors. Life in the workshops, streets, and bars cannot be reduced to work conditions or customs of lodging and eating. Everyday practices were the result of deliberation and strategizing, embedded in cultures constructed out of denial and submission, dreams and refusals, rational and considered choices, and above all a desire for legitimacy. The raw materials of the archive do allow for a limited reconstruction of the social landscape, but looking beyond this, there is the possibility of measuring and describing the gap that existed between the woman in the street and the image we see of her. Sometimes, in the answers given and the words spoken, there are unique moments where we can not only see routine day-to-day life, but glimpse what people thought about daily life. We can see ordinary men and women being in no way gullible, not about what they did, what they believed, or even what they asserted. These are privileged moments, and the richness of the archive lies in its ability to take us beyond simple descriptions of society. Through the documents we can come to understand how a population thought about itself, and how individuals constantly produced knowledge and understanding as they sought to find meaning that they both discovered and created over the course of the situations they experienced. Even if the elites were the only members of society who had the leisure to express themselves, and the pleasure of expressing themselves through writing, they were decidedly not the only ones to have a culture or a conflicted and complex view of themselves.[19]

Just because the popular classes were less adept at wielding the written word does not mean that they lived without constructing representations of themselves. The archive has many resources in this vein, and you need only take the trouble to look for them. It is too easy to find nothing more than a cumulative sum of attitudes; one must search for the systems of rationality that governed these attitudes. You must parse the words for something more than simple description of living conditions, and reject the notion that a popular culture is nothing more than attitudes, behaviors, and reactions. Its scope is far greater than this.

The archive retraces the insights that were behind individual behaviors and judgments, as well as the collective intelligence of groups. Once we have these, our work consists of identifying modes of reasoning, finding their rules, and picking out behaviors that devised their own meanings. This will allow us to understand the systems of reasoning and emotion that underlay both social cohesion and social conflict. In other words, it is a question of examining the distance that the individual places between her and herself, her and her behavior, her and the presentation of her behavior.

This is not easy because the judicial archives, like a microscope, reflect and magnify the conviction of governments and elites that it was impossible for the people to take part in public affairs or be actors in history. And yet, there is a large section of the police archives whose very contents contradict their certainty that popular opinion was entirely vacuous. The archives in question are those of the lieutenant general of Paris.[20] They contain the reports of the observers and inspectors[21] of the secret police that were called *gazetins*—little newspapers.

So suppose the people had neither judgments nor opinions, only notions and superstitions. Why then create an entire police force dedicated to capturing the murmurs and noises of the city, observing the streets and the rumors that rippled their surfaces? This is the paradoxical eighteenth century, which was founded on the exclusion of popular opinion, but operated under the impossible vision of being able to capture every move of its irregular and roiling flow. That the people have no business in politics was proclaimed from all sides. The lively debate about whether or not public opinion was important referred only to the opinions of the most enlightened circles,[22] leaving aside the idea of a popular opinion,[23] which, according to Condorcet, "is that of the stupidest and most miserable portion of the population." The belief that popular thought was inane was founded on the assumption that because the lower classes suffered the hardships of labor and want, they had neither the possibility nor the opportunity to bother themselves with anything that was not directly linked to their physical or material needs.

The form and content of the archives of the lieutenant general of police provide a double refutation of this self-satisfied philosophy. The creation of these archives in the first place reveals just how preoccupied the monarchy was with the rustling voices of the population. The weekly meetings between the lieutenant general of the police and the king are further proof of this. Moreover, it was in an effort to provide the monarch with as much information as possible that the lieutenant general had his entire network of informants and *mouches*[24]—"flies" on the wall—draw up detailed reports documenting the remarks they overheard while eavesdropping on crowds in public squares and on street corners throughout the city. Of course, we must be sure not to misinterpret this: being alert to the hubbub of the crowds is not the same thing as recognizing the people as a legitimate interlocutor. But, on the other hand, we cannot deny that this incessant, almost obsessive, pursuit influenced political decisions.[25] The structure of the police organization itself was shaped around the daily need to know and hear everything, and the way in which the lieutenant general's archives were assembled reflects this frenzied preoccupation with detail, to the point that they were indiscriminately recording words spoken at random in public conversations.

The contents of the reports written by the observers recording their strolls through the city mirror their intentions. One should not hope to find an organized and thematic narrative of popular opinions on the great events of the day in these letters and loose sheets that were only later bound together. Rather, these notes are the disorderly echo of the disorder perceived by their authors. Here, everything is fleeting: the rumor overheard, the idle talk around the city, the comment made out to be seditious. All of these were recorded by a fast-moving quill, whose only rhythm was the occurrence of events and reactions to them. There is no style, no structure, no trace of eloquence. This is an archive that tried to follow the fleeting stream of conversations but never sorted them out and rarely, if ever, named its sources: "It is said that . . . we heard that . . . there is a lot of noise about. . . ." Official notices are there as well, in their proper place: news of wars, of the church, and of princes' travels. But they do not dominate the other noises; they are side by side with a conversation overheard in a tavern or a peddler's echoing cry. It may seem as if nothing was left out, but we cannot know this for sure. In any case, nothing is presented as more important than anything else, and nothing was deemed too trivial to be jotted down. The reports pass from one subject to another, without proving anything and without surprise. Swamped in news, the observer, strained for information and pressed for time, reproduced on the spur of the moment the sudden and impetuous events of city life.

This archive, this collection of the secret police's gazetins, is both intriguing and contradictory. It puts on display the complexity of a monarchical system that sought to eradicate the popular sphere, while at the same time constantly seeking out popular beliefs and emotions. In search of popular approval, the royal propaganda campaign feverishly fed itself on that which was furthest from approval. This system denied any value to popular opinion when it became critical, yet still pursued any signs of such criticism so stubbornly that one might say, paradoxically, that it kindled and fueled them. Considered significant if they were contented, but deemed dark, vain, and enigmatic if they were angry, can the words of the people, as seen by a police force whose sole responsibility was keeping tabs on them, become a means of gaining access to representations of the "muffled plebeian public sphere" that Jürgen Habermas has argued remained out of reach throughout the eighteenth century, except in the space of an instant at the beginning of the French Revolution?

It is certainly a challenge to try and find in these archives a way of thinking about what politics meant in a society that knew nothing of the procedures that characterize politics, a society that denied its people even the idea that they could have opinions, asking them only to cheer or at least to refrain from any uprising. It is certainly a challenge to classify the conversations overheard by a police force avid for gossip as political speech. But it is a risk worth taking, because it is in this world of fragmented speech that everyday social experience takes shape. It takes shape through the words that articulate the reasonings of people who were not considered to be capable of reason. In this way, we can catch sight of the way events were interpreted, identify opinions and judgments as they were articulated through systems of representations, and uncover the subtle ways political and social knowledge were expressed, in which actions were improvised and individuals took advantage of the moment at hand in order to make new demands. Here, the archive contains what it rejects: the close attention the lower classes paid to questions and debates that the authorities tried to hide from them, but which they considered meaningful. Wouldn't we call this political judgment?

Here again, we must work with the scattered echoes and pieces of news recorded in the archive, whose fragmentation is less a lacuna than the reflection of a mode of being. There are specific moments where the words begin to jostle each other, where their outpouring floods the observers' reports and where those observers began to feel uncharacteristically uneasy in the face of so much vigor, rowdiness, and clamor, especially as speech was followed and reinforced by writings. Posters, pamphlets, and broadsheets invaded the streets, giving voices other ways of being expressed and transmitted.

The brisk back and forth between the written and the spoken word swayed the city to its rhythm. A good example of this is the affair of the *convulsionnaires* of the Cemetery of Saint-Médard, which, between 1730 and 1736, warranted almost round-the-clock attention from the mouches.[26] First of all, there were the agents charged with collecting in full detail the dreams, pronouncements, and prophesies of the convulsionnaires themselves.[27] Then there were all of the informants who recorded what was being said about the affair in public squares and on street corners. A brief reminder of the facts: in 1728, Cardinal Fleury, minister of the king, launched a heavy offensive against the Jansenists, and by 1730 three hundred clergymen had been banned. Meanwhile, strange things were happening inside the walled cemetery of the Saint-Médard church. A deacon named Pâris had lived there, dedicating himself entirely to asceticism and poverty, and sleeping in a shack at the heart of the poor neighborhood of Faubourg Saint-Marcel. Up until his death in 1727 he remained opposed to the Constitution and to Rome. He was beloved by his congregation, and his death led to several demonstrations, which were, at first, very discreet. People began gathering in groups and praying at his grave. This was followed by several miracles and several miraculous recoveries, the news of which was passed on discreetly by word of mouth, rather than openly discussed. This phenomenon grew as the royal repression spread, and, after a wave of arrests that took in 250 convulsionnaires, a royal decision was made, on the 27th of January 1732, to close the cemetery. From this date forward, the gazetins were bursting with reactions: "Paris is flooded with writings . . . we hear of nothing else besides . . . the picklocks are shouting that . . . everywhere people are speaking of . . . people are saying loudly and forcefully . . ."

But what is being said? Something fell into place and took shape around this event, and we must recognize its outlines. The roar of the rumors is deafening and the words uttered inside the cemetery walls carried so much weight that the Jansenist newspaper *Les Nouvelles ecclésiastiques* published them. This gave them a new power, pushing aside for the first time the idea that popular opinion belonged alongside fables and superstitions, not in serious newspapers. But let us return to the archival texts and the words that were transcribed at this precise moment. We should take note of how something specific came to be created around a location—the cemetery—and we should also notice how a space can give rise to events and shape them.

The cemetery was a familiar place. Located right in the middle of urban life, it represented a kind of shared community between living and dead. For this reason, the cemetery was also a place of imaginary evocations, fantasies, and collective fears, a place where anything was possible. Strange sounds were heard at night, vapors rose up from the ground, and corpses were stolen for morbid transactions. And what should we make of those who were so afraid of being buried alive that they asked to be outfitted with little bells before embarking on the final voyage, just in case? It was a familiar and yet uncertain place, but above all it was sacred ground. The king's decision to close it and place a prohibition upon it was seen by the population as a sort of crime of lèse-majesté, which is rather the height of irony for a king. The cemetery was fundamentally a place of God, and that He produced miracles there should force the king to back down. Observers noted the scandalized remarks that could be overheard throughout the city, "that it is unheard of for a king to go so far as to interfere with the miracles of God," "that it is indecent to have archers guarding the doors of a cathedral and a cemetery," "that proceeding in this manner dishonors the king as well as religion," "that it is scandalous that the officers swear and utter the words B*** and F***, that they must respect the fact that the cemetery is a holy place," and "that thunderous punishment will befall the king and Fleury."[28]

On top of these scandalized comments, people told stories, each one assuring that this or that really happened,

Captured Speech

each episode further proof of the ignominy of the royal order. The closing of the cemetery represented a flouting of death, and in response there was an active death that struck down those who guarded the cemetery. Strange events were whispered here and there, attaching the specter of sudden death to those who were involved in the closing of the cemetery. "People are saying," reported the *gazetins*, "that there are two archers who died suddenly in the cemetery, for having committed some or other irreverent act, and that they were buried on the spot in silence." "People are saying that the lieutenant general of the police travelled to Saint-Médard at midnight, accompanied by two masons, to exhume the body of Father Pâris, and that one of the masons fell stone dead as he was about to break ground with his mattock and that the other, who they are saying was named Serviat, died suddenly a few days later." And again: "It is said that prelates are dying suddenly as punishment for their villainy." Some even evoke the death of the king, and this possibility is confirmed by the death of the Duke of Anjou, his son.

In the public mind, fair is fair: their banishment from sacred burial grounds warrants severe punishment. And sudden death is an especially brutal punishment, for a very specific reason. In the eighteenth century, sudden death was a definitive manifestation of God's disapproval, because it denied someone the time to repent and confess.[29] Sudden death was nothing less than the hand of God.

A whirlwind of harsh words and severe criticisms was amplified and authenticated through unverifiable stories whispered inside taverns and across alleyways. These stories made use of all the same themes, and strung one after another they left no doubt that the king was wrong, God had proved it.

There is often a similarity between the way some important event in the social life of the city was discussed and the contents of the most sensational news stories of the time. It is as if the mass of loose papers sold in the streets, full of marvels and catastrophes, in one way or another provided the stories that allowed people to think about events. There is almost never a word-for-word similarity between religious, economic, and political news and the sensational broadsheets, but there was a process of connections through which the population, who did not have direct access to these events, sought to narrate them with the tools they had at hand, mining the sensational news stories for an allegorical and colorful repertoire that could not only bridge this gap, but also legitimate their convictions and found their truths.

The judicial archive in this instance contains a fascinating combination of what it denied and what it wanted at all costs to hear. The words hunted down, the stories that people told each other and themselves, the way in which the occupation of a public space could incite people to action, as well as representations and acts as they were being improvised, all fit together as forms of social knowledge and recognizable modes of popular expression. They represent history as it was being constructed, when the outcome was never entirely clear. To understand them, you must leave behind the received wisdom of hindsight that claims to be able to classify certain beliefs and behaviors as archaic, others as modern. You must instead trace the paths of actors who improvised their forms of behavior as they went along, not only participating in events but also fighting to find meaning in them, despite all of the attempts from on high to keep them in the dark. When a reader in the archives examines what happened during an event, she tells it and undoes it at the same time, taking care not to water it down or negate it, without superimposing "her" meaning on the one that the historical actors were always searching for inside the event itself. Through the archive we can glimpse what became of these people who were constantly in movement, and whose agency was composed of a continual combination and recombination of action and reaction, change and conflict. We must seize on to what happened, recognizing that in the facts we find in the archive something was always going on inside social relationships. As we abandon abstract categorizations, we can bring to light something that moved, arose, and fulfilled itself through continual change.

The Inventory Room
Is Sepulchral

The inventory room is sepulchral. Someone decided that central heating wasn't needed here, so cold damp air is continually drifting down from the high ceilings. Prison-issue gray iron tables line the length of walls stacked high with volumes. Their purpose is to allow for the consultation of the inventories that contain the serial numbers under which a sought-after document is stored. In the middle of the room there is a table, as austere as the others, although perhaps slightly larger. An impassive archivist is sitting there. Beside a window opening on to the garden, a staff person is numbering pages in diligent handwriting. Not a single word can be heard; there are only a few rare smiles and vague whispers. The shuffling of papers is monotonous, and the clock above the double-hinged door no longer tells time. Time is elsewhere, as the clock has been still for a long time, like the one in the porphyry room of the Escorial where the kings and queens of Spain are buried, sternly laid out in their marble tombs. At the bottom of that dark Spanish valley the long line of the monarchy lies at rest; at the bottom of the Marais in Paris the traces of the past lie at rest. An analogy between the two mausoleums may seem arbitrary, yet on each of her visits to the inventory room she is struck by this memory from across the Pyrenees.

Today, an intimidated young man is asking the archivist on duty for advice. He would like to compile his family's genealogy for his ailing father. The oppressive strictness of the inventory room has slightly stooped his shoulders, perhaps even more so than usual. Awkwardly hanging on to his brown leather briefcase, he almost doesn't dare look in the direction being indicated to him. The archivist, speaking very quietly, takes out a volume from behind him, and, with his fingertips, traces the printed lines of numbers preceded by capital letters. Then, softly, he leads the young man to the long row where the indexes are kept. He takes down six or seven volumes, picking them out without hesitation. He opens them up, points to the long columns of numbers, closes them, puts down the books, picks up others, explains, and returns to his desk to consult a set of file cards tightly squeezed into a beige shoe box. The young man listens, briefcase in hand, with the expression on his face of a traveler who finds himself in an unfamiliar neighborhood of a foreign city and has no idea how much longer it will take to reach his destination. The hands of the clock hang motionless. The archivist returns to where the young man is standing, whispers a few words into his ear, and abandons him at the table on which the books are laid out. The young man sits down, begins to read, and removes a white piece of paper from his briefcase, which he has finally released from his grasp. His eyes wander from one page to the next without fixing on anything, once or twice lifting to observe the other readers who, green squares in hand, only come here to quickly double-check a reference. It seems as though he envies them, she thinks. He remains in this spot taking notes for a long time. His white sheet becomes dark with serial numbers written at an increasingly fevered pace. He is at the entrance to a long labyrinth into which he is descending with a heavy step, less worried about the eventual exit than the web of paper streets through which he will have to walk.

The inventory room of the National Archives is nothing like the reference rooms or card catalogues of other libraries, which are energetic and animated, and whose wooden drawers can be closed as briskly as they were opened if you fail to find the desired

The Inventory Room Is Sepulchral

reference. Their bright wood is not in mourning, and their readers, looking relaxed, use this break to stretch their backs and keep each other up to date on the latest news of the academic world. In those card catalogues, it is not frowned upon to walk around with pencil in your mouth, three blank pages in hand, high heels clicking crisply on the floor. These rooms are an amusing sight; instead of the galley-slaves, backs bent, hunched over and silent, that you see in reading rooms, you have a view that is charmingly out of the ordinary; the disembodied heads of men and women floating above the tops of filing cabinets. People do not talk loudly, but not exactly quietly either. In certain libraries raised filing cabinets give a view of researchers' legs, sometimes stiff and alert, sometimes relaxed.

In the inventory room, by contrast, the world stands still, stiff as a statue. The index books are sibylline to anyone who does not know their code. Breathing quietly, each person hunts for the magic words that will open the door to them, although only one door at a time, of course. In a library, the right call number to the right book will sometimes give the researcher a definitive answer on the spot. An archival reference number, however, often will only direct the reader to another serial number that will itself only give access to a new series where other serial numbers await. Your eyes become glazed over from having to memorize this immense world that spans not just from A to Z but from Z^{1A} to Z^{1H}. Secrets are there to be found, but are sometimes impossibly out of reach. An old hand's pride rests on derisory victories; when he encounters another veteran, he might, *casually, mention in conversation that Y 10139 is significantly better preserved than X²ᴮ 1354. In the inventory room he is no longer a man in a tomb, but a fish in an aquarium. We can observe this evolution when, a month later, the same young man enters, relaxed and smiling, and quickly heads toward a large crimson volume that he immediately opens to the right page. He copies down two pieces of information, straightens his shoulders, and looks distractedly at the clock that still refuses to budge. Satisfied, he puts back the inventory, and, as he heads back to the reading room where the manuscripts are waiting, he notices a timid young man, slightly hunched over, not daring to disturb the archivist. He turns away briskly, then closes the door behind him. In the hallway he runs into a friend whom he first met in this pale white room. He announces happily that he will soon be able to give his father the eagerly anticipated genealogy. He adds, who knows why, that this summer he is heading back to the Escorial to see the royal tombs. . . . She smiles.*

Everything goes on around the woman at the head of the room, and everything must go through her. The raised platform where her desk sits, and which gives the reading room its distinctive appearance, is surrounded by incessant sound and agitation. Ordinarily, things would be calm and the room would have its unmistakable smell, a mixture of wax and the light fragrance of faded leather bindings. But nothing looks as it did the day before, and as soon as one enters the room a smell of peppery perfume sets the tone. There is no doubt:

The Inventory Room Is Sepulchral

today is the day that she presides over the reading room. She is like a baroque queen in heavy jewels and a garish flower-print dress; her perfume is as overpowering as the wind at low tide. No one can escape it, except perhaps for the last few rows in the back, farthest away and therefore best protected. It is clear from the raised heads, the hands flipping through pages with exasperation, and the feet twisted tensely around the legs of chairs that the first rows are in turmoil, inescapably contaminated by her severe and imposing demeanor. She reigns, gives advice that bears a strong resemblance to orders, speaks very loudly, and does not understand what she does not wish to understand, all the while constantly ruffling the pages of her morning newspaper. At times, an article she reads makes her sigh or grumble, it's often hard to tell which. There is nothing to be gained from disturbing her at this time; it is better to take your distance, head over to where the current periodicals are kept, and dive into a semi-recent magazine. You will only come back when a vague smile will have made her seem almost gentle.

Five or six times a morning, eight or nine times an afternoon, she receives a phone call on a phone that is not on her desk. Therefore, a staff person must gesture to her from across the room, miming holding up a phone and mouthing "TELEPHONE." These silent lips on the other side of the room have an effect on her similar to that of a catapult. She does not stand up, she leaps up, both arms pushing on her desk to better take off. She sweeps down the two steps like a bursting dam, and is on her way. Is she trying to go as quickly as possible or make as little noise as possible? She is waddling curiously on her tiptoes so that she is not exactly running, only half moving her hips, striking the floor with tiny clicks. This scene, in this paneled and studious reading room, is like a cataclysm. She quickens her pace as she nears the room with the telephone, keeping her balance by bracing herself on a long table, before pivoting around the corner and continuing her race. The porter took the precaution of leaving the door open, and in a final slide that shakes the expertly pinned bun in her hair, she reaches her goal, both arms outstretched. The door closes and a few pieces of paper take flight in her wake. You can hear her piercing voice falling into sugary politeness, without quite being able to make out the actual content of the conversation. All eyes in the room reapply themselves to files and registers, trying to regain their concentration, forgetting that this precipitous voyage will necessarily have a return leg. It unfolds in the same manner: catastrophically. She does not climb up the two steps as much as she swallows them, before sitting down noisily and beginning to almost yell at the readers patiently waiting for her, dazedly holding out their squares, that she is not to be bothered with such small details. She is without peer.

Tomorrow, she won't be there, and she will be missed. The room will be almost too calm, too concentrated, one will have to try not to doze off. Luckily, the old Englishman in the third row will be there. As usual, he will inadvertently slam his desk closed. Every pair of shoulders in the room will jump in unison.

The Inventory Room Is Sepulchral

Writing

We cannot bring back to life those whom we find cast ashore in the archives. But this is not a reason to make them suffer a second death. There is only a narrow space in which to develop a story that will neither cancel out nor dissolve these lives, but leave them available so that another day, and elsewhere, another narrative can be built from their enigmatic presence.

A taste for these ragged tatters of words and actions will always shape the way you write about them. Grounded in fragments, this style of writing builds on sequences of what was plausible, rather than what was necessarily true. Historians must search for a language that will allow us to bring unexpected new pieces of knowledge to light, while accepting that certain things will remain unknowable. Attempting to fashion history out of what might have happened is a perilous undertaking, as we try to discern the unstable order of things through the clutter of everyday events, which itself makes one or another scenario probable or improbable.

To do this properly, we must distance ourselves from the idea of the archive as a reflection—the view that we can only extract facts from it—as well as the idea of the archive as conclusive proof, which presumes that we can pin down once and for all the meaning of the documents. So how can we invent a language that will grasp what we are looking for here, among these infinite traces of challenges, reversals, and successes? Well, even if the words we use do not permit the acts they describe to be played again, they can at least evoke alternate outcomes, margins of freedom for possible futures, if only by conveying a sense of human dignity and working to measure the depth of sorrow and pain. Of course, as Paul Ricœur has written, "history only emerges after the game has already been played."[1] But historical writing should retain the hint of the unfinished, giving rein to freedoms even after they were scorned, refusing to seal off or conclude anything, and always avoiding received wisdom. It should be possible to find new ways of bending our words to the rhythm of the surprises experienced when in dialogue with the archives, forcing them to partner with intellectual hesitation so that we can see both crimes and desires for emancipation as they appeared in the moment, holding on to the possibility that each would be wedded later on to other dreams and other visions. There is surely a way, through nothing more than the choice of words, to produce tremors, to break through the obvious, and to outflank the ordinary smooth course of scientific knowledge. There is surely a way to go beyond the drab restitution of an event or a historical subject, and mark the places where meaning was undone, producing gaps where certainty had once reigned. Stretched between the need to create meaning through a narrative that fits together, and the insistence that nothing should be reified, historical writing must chart a course between understanding and reason, passion and disorder.

Now, as we reach the end of the book, this perspective is no secret. The allure of the archives entails a roaming voyage through the words of others, and a search for a language that can rescue their relevance. It may also entail a voyage through the words of today, with the perhaps somewhat unreasonable conviction that we write history not just to tell it, but to anchor a departed past to our words and bring about an "exchange among the living."[2] We write to enter into an unending conversation about humanity and forgetting, origins and death. About the words each of us uses to enter into the debates that surround us.

Notes

Chapter 1: Traces by the Thousands

1. To avoid lengthy and unnecessary repetitions, from here on "archives" will stand in for "judicial archives."

2. "Relations" were broadsheets that told stories of sensational or sordid news, marvels, and miscellaneous curiosities, and were hawked on the streets in the eighteenth century.

3. Jacques André, "De la preuve à l'histoire, les archives en France," *Traverses* 36 (January 1986): 29.

4. In the Archives of France in 1980, a growth of seventy-five kilometers each year was reported; cf. André, "De la preuve à l'histoire," 27.

5. In the Archives of the Bastille one can find countless police files about printers, vendors, and employees of booksellers who were imprisoned for having printed and sold pamphlets and defamatory broadsheets.

6. Philippe Lejeune, *On Autobiography* (Le Pacte autobiographique), ed. Paul John Eakin, trans. Katherine Leary (Minneapolis: University of Minnesota Press, 1989).

7. Bibliothèque de l'Arsenal (hereafter B.A.), Archives de la Bastille (hereafter A.B.), 12057, July 8, 1759.

8. Bibliothèque de l'Académie de médecine, SRM 179, the case of Anne Barbaroux, 1785; cf. also Jean-Pierre Peter, "Entre femmes

et médecins: Violences et singularités dans le discours du corps d'après les manuscrits médicaux de la fin du XVIIIe siècle," *Ethnologie française* 6, no. 3–4 (1976).

9. Historian's jargon meaning to come home after working in the archives.

Chapter 2: Paths and Presences

1. Louis-Sébastien Mercier, *Tableau de Paris*, 12 vols. (Amsterdam, 1782).

2. Nicolas Rétif de la Bretonne, *Les Nuits de Paris*, 2 vols. (Paris, 1930).

3. Arlette Farge and Michel Foucault, *Le Désordre de familles, les lettres de cachet des Archives de la Bastille* (Paris: Gallimard, 1982).

4. These are names of punishments incurred in the eighteenth century, and we might add to these the stocks, and banishment, where the delinquent is ordered to leave his or her province.

5. Natalie Zemon Davis, *Fiction in the Archives: Pardon Tales and Their Tellers in Sixteenth-Century France* (Stanford, Calif.: Stanford University Press, 1987).

6. Michel Foucault, "La vie des hommes infâmes," *Cahiers du chemin* no. 29 (January 15, 1977): 13.

7. Foucault, "La vie des hommes."

8. Rudolf Dekker, "Women in Revolt: Popular Protest and Its Social Basis in Holland in the XVIIth and XVIIIth century," *Theory and Society* 16 (1987).

9. A *chambrelan* was self-employed and worked from the home without belonging to the formal community of a trade. This was a marginal activity that was severely punished by the labor police.

10. Archives Nationales (hereafter A.N.), AD III 7, October 16, 1749, in Saint-Arnoult (election de Beauvais).

11. Among the documents of the Bibliothèque Bleue, for example, there are numerous attacks on women; cf. Arlette Farge, *Le Miroir des femmes, textes de la Bibliothèque bleue* (Paris: Editions Montalbe, 1982).

12. Arlette Farge, "Les femmes, la violence et le sang au XVIIIe siècle," *Mentalités* 1 (September 1988).

13. Natalie Zemon Davis, *Society and Culture in Early Modern France: Eight Essays* (Stanford, Calif.: Stanford University Press, 1975).

14. Cf. Claude Mettra, "Le ventre et son royaume," *L'Arc* no. 52 (1972): 38.

Chapter 3: Gathering and Handling the Documents

1. See especially Robert Mandrou and Michel de Certeau, as well as Philippe Ariès, Michel Foucault, and Jacques Rancière.

2. All of which are stored at the B.A.

3. A.B. 10019.

4. Affaire Thorin, 1758, A.B. 12023.

5. Pierre Retat, *L'Attentat de Damiens: Discours sur l'événement au XVIIIe siècle* (Lyon: Presse universitaires de Lyon, 1979).

6. Michel de Certeau, *The Writing of History* (L'Écriture de l'histoire), trans. Tom Conley (New York: Columbia University Press, 1992).

7. A.N., Y 13728 s.d.

8. A.N., Y 10999 to Y 11032, superintendent Hugues, neighborhood of Les Halles, 1757 to 1788.

9. A.N., Y11007^A, superintendent Hugues.

10. Carlo Ginzburg and Carlo Poni, "La Micro-histoire," *Le Débat* 17 (December 1981): 133.

Chapter 4: Captured Speech

1. A.N., X^{2B} 1367, June 1750.

2. Erving Goffman, *Forms of Talk* (Philadelphia: University of Pennsylvania Press, 1981).

3. Arlette Farge and Jacques Revel, *The Vanishing Children of Paris: Rumor and Politics Before the French Revolution* (Logiques de la foule: L'affaire des enlèvements d'enfants, Paris, 1750), trans. Claudia Mieville (Cambridge: Harvard University Press, 1991).

4. A.B. 11929, year 1757.

5. A.B. 11923, year 1756.

6. A.N. X²ᴮ 1367, year 1750.

7. Carlo Ginzburg, *The Cheese and the Worms: The Cosmos of a Sixteenth-Century Miller* (Le Fromage et les vers: L'univers d'un meunier au XVIe siècle), trans. John and Anne C. Tedeschi (Baltimore: Johns Hopkins University Press, 1992).

8. Michel Foucault, *The Order of Things: An Archeology of the Human Sciences* (London: Routledge Classics, 2002).

9. F. Dosse, "Foucault face à l'histoire," *Espace-Temps* 30: 14.

10. Jacques Revel, "Une œuvre inimitable," *Espace-Temps*, Braudel dans tous ses états, p. 14.

11. Edward Hallett Carr, *What Is History?* (New York: Random House, 1961), 16.

12. Interview with Lucette Finas, quoted in Maurice Blanchot, *Michel Foucault as I Imagine Him* (New York: Zone Books, 1997), 86.

13. Pierre Vidal-Naquet, *Assassins of Memory: Essays on the Denial of the Holocaust* (Les Assasins de la mémoire), trans. Jeffrey Mehlman (New York: Columbia University Press, 1993).

14. Pierre Vidal-Naquet, "Lettre," Michel de Certeau, Centre G. Pompidou, 1987, pp. 71–72.

15. It is with Mr. Ricœur's permission that I cite his words from oral remarks made during the colloquium "About Paul Ricœur," organized by Roger Chartier and Francois Hartog for the École des hautes etudes en sciences sociales, June 22, 1988.

16. Here I cite the words of Mr. Chartier from his comments, June 22, 1988.

17. Vidal-Naquet, *Assassins of Memory*.

18. Carr, *What Is History?* 22.

19. Jacques Rancière, *The Nights of Labor: The Workers' Dream in Nineteenth-Century France* (La Nuit des prolétaires: Archives du rêve ouvrier), trans. John Drury (Philadelphia: Temple University Press, 1991).

20. The position of lieutenant general of the police was created in Paris in 1667. The entire police force was organized under his authority. These archives are primarily stored in the Bibliothèque de l'Arsenal.

21. A.B. 10155 to 10170, years 1724–1781.

22. Jürgen Habermas, *L'Espace public, archéologie de la publicité comme dimension constitutive de la société bourgeoise* (Paris: Payot, 1978).

23. On the theme of public opinion in the eighteenth century, see the works of Keith Baker, "Politique et opinion publique sous l'Ancien Régime," *Annales ESC* (January–February 1987); Roger Chartier, "Culture populaire et culture politique sous l'Ancien Régime," in *French Revolution and the Creation of Modern Political Culture*, vol. 1, *Political Culture of the Ancient Regime* (Oxford: Pergamon Press, 1987); Sarah Maza, "Le Tribunal de la nation: Memoires judiciaires et l'opinion publique à la fin de l'Ancien Régime," *Annales ESC* (January–February 1987); Mona Ozouf, "L'opinion publique," in *Political Culture of the Ancient Regime* (Oxford: Pergamon Press, 1987); Jean Sgard, "Naissance de l'opinion publique," in *Lumen* 7, Man and Nature/l'Homme et la Nature, pp. 1–11.

24. *Mouche*—meaning fly—was the name given to the undercover police observers who monitored crowds and public spaces.

25. On the police's obsession with collecting rumors and words, cf. the intelligence dossiers stored at the Arsenal Library in the Archives of the Bastille that concern contemporary affairs (the Jansénistes affair, surveillance of morals, gambling houses, surveillance of foreigners, et cetera).

26. Cathérine-Laurence Maire, *Les Convulsionnaires de Saint-Médard* (Paris: Gallimard, 1985); Daniel Vidal, *Miracles et Convulsions jansénistes au XVIIIe siècle* (Paris: PUF, 1987).

27. A.B. 10196–10206. Daily police reports on the goings-on at the Saint-Médard cathedral, 1720–1757.
28. A.B. 10161.
29. Robert Favre, *La Mort au siècle des Lumières* (Lyon: Presses universitaires de Lyon, 1978).

Chapter 5: Writing

1. Paul Ricœur, *Temps et récit* (Paris: Éditions du Seuil, 1983), vol. 1, p. 222.
2. Certeau, *L'Écriture de l'histoire*, 61.

Translator's Notes

a. The French word *fonds* can refer either to archival collections or to the ocean floor.
b. The French word *source* can refer to either sources of information or natural springs of water.
c. The term *Histoire des mentalités*, literally "history of mentalities," was particularly associated in the 1970s and 1980s with work inspired by the examples of Robert Mandrou, Georges Duby, and Jacques Le Goff, among others.
d. The author uses the French word *dépouiller*, which is the standard term for the process of unpacking the archival bundles and sifting through documents. It has its roots in words for undressing or unveiling, skinning an animal, and pillaging.